C000226672

"A master of fiction, Jill Eileen Sr
in the world of Christian writing,
such as the Wives of King David,
Daughters of the Promised Land. In her work, she expertly
combines her biblical research with her fiction writing skills
and brings three-thousand-year-old characters to life for her
readers. Now, Smith branches into the world of nonfiction
with her new title, *She Walked Before Us*, researching famous
women of the Bible in-depth and pulling lessons from their
lives for the growth of women today. The book is sure to be
a page-turner and a life-changer!"

Angelia L. White, creator and founder of *Hope for Women*
magazine; author of *Yes Sisters*

"In this captivating book, Jill Eileen Smith brings the biblical
stories of twelve women to life with thought-provoking clarity.
She invites us to step into the flesh-and-bone reality of each
woman, then carefully walks alongside us on each journey as
a trusted guide, offering wisdom and practical encouragement
in the midst of their disappointment, despair, delight, and
doubt. Far more than a Bible study, *She Walked Before Us* is a
powerful and meaningful bridge that connects us to a heritage
of hope and redemption."

Ronne Rock, storyteller, speaker, and author
of *One Woman Can Change the World*

"In *She Walked Before Us*, Jill Eileen Smith walks readers through
the lives of twelve Old Testament women, giving voice to their
stories in fresh, new ways. By adding her own experience and
thought-provoking questions, Smith illuminates the path for
modern women, leading us through difficult challenges into
victory and joy."

Gwen Ford Faulkenberry, author of *Jesus, Be Near Me*
and *A Beautiful Life*; coauthor *of Mornings with Jesus*

"Have you ever found yourself feeling common or typical? Do you feel your life is just run-of-the-mill? Or do you ever think you aren't special or unique, and you wonder how God could use a person like you? Well, I invite you to come along on an adventure with award-winning author Jill Eileen Smith as she shares the captivating accounts of twelve ordinary women from the Old Testament. Through the challenging terrain of Scripture, Smith helps her readers unearth nuggets of truth from women in the past who have left footprints that guide our way today. If you have been challenged by the changing seasons in your life and wonder how your unknown future could ever follow God's plan, then let yourself be surprised and, yes, exhilarated by God's leading."

**Dorothy Valcarcel**, founder of crosswalk.com

# She Walked Before Us

# Previous books by Jill Eileen Smith

### The Wives of King David

*Michal*

*Abigail*

*Bathsheba*

### Wives of the Patriarchs

*Sarai*

*Rebekah*

*Rachel*

### Daughters of the Promised Land

*The Crimson Cord*

*The Prophetess*

*Redeeming Grace*

*A Passionate Hope*

*The Heart of a King*

*Star of Persia*

*When Life Doesn't Match Your Dreams*

*She Walked Before Us*

# She Walked Before Us

Grace, Courage, and Strength

from 12 Women

of the Old Testament

## JILL EILEEN SMITH

### Revell

a division of Baker Publishing Group
Grand Rapids, Michigan

© 2020 by Jill E. Smith

Published by Revell
a division of Baker Publishing Group
PO Box 6287, Grand Rapids, MI 49516-6287
www.revellbooks.com

Printed in the United States of America

Library of Congress Cataloging-in-Publication Data
Names: Smith, Jill Eileen, 1958– author.
Title: She walked before us : grace, courage, and strength from 12 women of the Old Testament / Jill Eileen Smith.
Description: Grand Rapids, Michigan : Revell, [2020]
Identifiers: LCCN 2019056068 | ISBN 9780800728687 (paperback)
Subjects: LCSH: Christian women—Religious life. | Women in the Bible—Biography. | Bible. Old Testament—Biography.
Classification: LCC BV4527 .S6284 2020 | DDC 221.9/22082—dc23
LC record available at https://lccn.loc.gov/2019056068

ISBN 978-0-8007-3988-1 (hardcover)

Published in association with Books & Such Literary Management, 5926 Sunhawk Dr., Santa Rosa, CA 95409, www.booksandsuch.com.

20 21 22 23 24 25 26    7 6 5 4 3 2 1

green
press
INITIATIVE

To every person who has faced
life's trials, run into the brick wall
of immovable circumstances,
and found a way by God's grace
to walk through in victory—
these stories are for you.

# CONTENTS

# INTRODUCTION

In 2019, *When Life Doesn't Match Your Dreams* released as the first volume in this nonfiction collection. I didn't know what to expect from nonfiction, as it is very different from my novels. The interest in that book and the comments from readers who wrote and told me how it touched their hearts have blessed me more than I can express. Perhaps the human condition and emotions we feel are more similar than we know.

As we embark on this second edition of biblical women, I hope that whatever you are facing in your life right now, you can give it to the Lord and look to Him for the victory. Like those in the first book, these women also faced great struggles, some far worse than I've ever known. But maybe you have known those feelings, tragedies, or fears.

In this book, we will see women who complained too much or wanted a husband who wasn't so angry. One had to accept a call from God she might not have wanted. Another lost much and gained more. One had to go back before she could go forward. Another had a great deal to forgive. Still another stood by helplessly as her son committed rape and was later murdered. And another had to deal with knowing her son had killed his brother.

How does one live through such things? And if we haven't experienced them, what lessons might God teach us along the way?

Through it all, I hope you see that in every trial, circumstance, lesson, heartache, or joy, God is there and He is not silent. You may not see what He is doing behind the scenes, but He never stops seeking you. He never stops loving you. And when you are caught in the middle, in the past, or in a deep pit, remember this—others have walked this path before you. When they cried out to God in humility and need, He listened. He is listening to you too, and calling your name. Do you hear Him?

I pray the stories of these women give you what you need to better know our great God and Savior Jesus Christ, whose story is woven into the lives of those born before He came to earth. Even in the lives of often forgotten women.

In His Grace,
Jill Eileen Smith

# Miriam

## When God Corrects Your Character

*(Based on Exodus 15; Numbers 12; 20:1)*

### If I Were Miriam

"With Your unfailing love You lead the people You have redeemed. In Your might, You guide them to Your sacred home." The words came easily from my lips that day, and my heart still sings them as I work about my tent. *Free*. Many times during my eighty-five years, I had wondered if I would live to see this day. Hadn't Ima and Abba suspected that Moses would lead us out of Egypt?

My feet move to the rhythm of my heart song as I mix flour with the water of Marah, which God has made sweet instead of bitter. How good is our God!

Sounds of singing whisper to me on the wind. The women of Israel still rejoice in the words Moses led us to sing once the Egyptian army perished in the sea. How is it possible? Freedom tastes strange. Sweet. We are used to the lash of the taskmasters or the restrictions on our movements, the constant fear that Pharaoh will do something else to make our lives more miserable than they already are . . . were.

A breeze filters through the tent as the flap lifts. I turn to smile at Elisheba, Aaron's wife. We are like sisters, she and I. I am grateful, for I do not know Moses's wife, Zipporah, yet. But Elisheba has been with us nearly as long as Jephunneh, my husband.

"Welcome," I say, moving closer to embrace her. We laugh. How good it feels to welcome her in freedom.

"I thought you could use some company." She sinks onto the floor and takes some of the grain to grind for me. My men will be eager to eat the moment they return from scouting the camp with Moses and Aaron.

"You are right. I always appreciate your company." I return to mixing the flour and water. "Do you ever feel strange?" I glance at her. "As though none of this is real?"

She nods. "Every moment. I mean, we knew it was coming. I never doubted that Moses and our God would triumph. But to be truly free, to see the Egyptian army destroyed, is something I will never forget."

"Nor I. But as a people, will we forget all of the miracles our God did in Egypt?" I search her face. "We have led the women for years, and we know how easy it is for them to fall back into despair. We grew so weary of waiting." I stop, remembering. How often had I encouraged even Elisheba to not lose hope? Will I still be needed in that role now that we are free?

"You are right, but in one sense, I think the women will remember far more what God has done for us than the fear and the losses we suffered in Egypt. How could we deny His power now? We have seen Him work with our own eyes! We have watched His powerful arm reach even into Pharaoh's own palace. How could we ever be unfaithful to Him now? Not after that." Elisheba lifts her chin in certainty.

I am too skeptical. I know this. "And yet the people complained against Moses just two days ago because the waters were bitter."

Elisheba stops grinding and tilts her head as if thinking. At last she nods. "You would think they would simply trust or ask Moses to pray for water. Aaron says the people were as bitter as the stream."

How well I remember. We had traveled three days in the wilderness, searching for water and finding none. When at last we found water at an oasis, no one could drink it. We named the place *Marah*, meaning "bitter." But Elisheba is right. Not even a week out of Egypt, and our people who were thirsty grew angry with my brother. Jephunneh told me how he and our sons had stood with Moses and Aaron, but they made a small force against the anger of hundreds of men.

"We must keep after the women to trust Moses's leading and not to complain to their husbands. When we complain, our men in turn will complain to Moses. If we are not careful, we will stop trusting our God in exactly the way we think we won't. There are already signs of it." I move from my work to sink down beside her. "Moses says that God is testing us. Surely the people will want to pass the test!"

It was Elisheba's turn to look at me, her dark eyes filled with skepticism. "I hope so, Miriam. I want to believe that we can keep hope alive among our women. I want to see us obey our God as much as you do. But now that you mention it, it is disconcerting that the men complained so easily after only a few days."

"We never lacked water in Egypt." The Nile was Egypt's life force.

"How long will our God let us wander before we reach the land He has promised to us? Aaron says the journey isn't long. But will we go straight there and take what belongs to us?"

"Not even Moses can answer that. But the journey shouldn't take more than a few weeks or perhaps a month. I only hope the people are ready for a battle once we get there. I do not think the Canaanites will give up their land without one." Our people are not prepared for war. They are untrained slaves, barely able to follow Moses, Aaron, and me as we lead them.

"Perhaps we should suggest to Moses to build an army. It would not hurt to start training. Especially now that we are in a comfortable place with water." Elisheba chewed on a fingernail, a habit she practiced when her ideas caused her worry.

"I will speak to him at the evening meal tonight. Or I will speak to Jephunneh and let him make the suggestion. Sometimes my brother prefers my husband's counsel over mine." That irked me often. Hadn't God also spoken through me? Hadn't I protected Moses's very life when he was a babe in arms? But it is better to let Jephunneh speak to him. As long as the thing is accomplished, it matters not the source.

The tent flap lifts again, and both of us turn to see the object of my musings enter.

"You're early." I rise to greet my husband with a kiss on the cheek.

"I'm here to tell you to pack what you can. We have one more day here, and then we will move out. Moses's orders." He glances at Elisheba. "I only came to tell you. I will be back later."

He leaves without giving me a chance to question him. Moses's orders. God must have told him to move us onward.

Perhaps we will make it to the Promised Land sooner than I expect. A little thrill passes through me as I exchange a glance with Elisheba. A smile creases her slightly wrinkled face.

"I am glad," she says, standing. "I cannot wait to feast my eyes on the beauty that awaits us." She touches my arm. "I best go and do as Jephunneh said."

I walk her to the door, and we hug. I watch her walk a few steps to the tent she shares with my brother Aaron. Though Jephunneh is of the tribe of Judah, he has chosen to keep us near my brothers, Israel's leaders. I am grateful, and I am proud that my children have the heritage of both Levi and Judah. Priests and kings are promised to come from them.

I turn to survey the tent, pushing those thoughts aside. I must focus on doing as my husband has said, not warring with the seeds of jealousy and pride or the very complaining I accuse others of doing. None of them will do me any good.

## What We Know

Miriam was the sister of Moses and Aaron, daughter of Amram and Jochebed. Her story is sprinkled through the pages of Scripture from Exodus to Numbers. She was the young girl who watched her brother's "ark" in the Nile, and when the Egyptian princess found him, Miriam boldly asked the princess if she needed a Hebrew midwife to care for him. This is probably Miriam's most famous accomplishment.

Scripture also tells us that she was a prophetess and that she led Israel along with her brothers. She and Aaron complained against Moses later in their journey in the wilderness because of his choice of a wife, and God condemned Miriam with leprosy for a week for speaking against His chosen servant. We also know she died near the waters of Meribah.

Other than this, we know very little about Miriam. The Bible does not give us a name of a husband or even tell us if she married. No children are listed. My choice to give her both is for the sake of story—strictly my imagination—and because most women of her day would have married.

We are not sure of her age at the time of Moses's birth, though I have found sources that suggest she was either five or seven years old. This makes her quite young to watch her brother's ark bobbing in the waters of the Nile.

Miriam was probably at least eighty-five years old when the Hebrews finally escaped Egypt. She sang along with Moses after crossing the Red Sea and led the people in praise because they were finally free.

This type of leading in worship might go along with her gift of prophecy (Exod. 15:20). We aren't sure when God called her, but His words in Micah 6:4 indicate that she and Aaron led the people with Moses: "For I brought you up from the land of Egypt and redeemed you from the house of slavery, and I sent before you Moses, Aaron, and Miriam."

Given that she was put in a position of leadership along with her brothers, how do you think that made her feel? Women in leadership was not common in ancient times, and the number of prophets exceeded that of prophetesses. Miriam was chosen and perhaps more gifted than we may realize.

Not all people in positions of leadership have the gifts or calling they need to fulfill those roles. Some seek positions for selfish reasons, and others who are called to leadership do not seek it or—like Gideon, who came much later—do not want it. We aren't told whether Miriam wanted to prophesy or lead her people alongside her brothers, but eventually, the role seemed to cause her a little too much pride and ended in complaining.

We are not told what Miriam prophesied, but the daunting task to help lead the people could not have been easy, considering the size of Israel. Yet Miriam seemed to struggle in her later years with God's apparent favoritism of Moses over her and Aaron. Do you ever wonder if she wanted more? I do, and this is why: she complained.

Oh, can I relate to that. Can't you? Are we ever truly satisfied with our lives? It seems like there is always something that comes up that can cause us to either become dissatisfied and complain or lean into God and trust what we don't understand. Gratitude is harder to cultivate than complaining.

What we don't quite know is what she complained about. The Bible says it had to do with Moses's marriage to a Cushite woman. Perhaps Miriam and Aaron were upset with his choice because she was not from the nation of Israel. But neither was Moses's first wife, Zipporah, who came from the land of Midian. And what they said had nothing to do with the Cushite: "Has the LORD indeed spoken only through Moses? Has he not spoken through us also?" (Num. 12:2).

Did they think Moses needed their permission about who to marry? Or could they have carried around a bit of jealousy at Moses's favored status? Though we later read that God has no favorites, there are times when He chooses to use or bless certain people because He wants to do so.

Still, Miriam had been singled out as a leader, so why the complaining in her old age? Did she wish she could push the boundaries and hold even more authority than she did? We do have examples in Scripture where God spoke to women over men. Rebekah, Deborah, and Manoah's wife all heard from God apart from their husbands. Jesus revealed that He was the Messiah first to a woman (the Samaritan woman), He showed His resurrected body first to a woman (Mary

Magdalene), and He welcomed women (Joanna, Susanna, another Mary, and more) into his company. The apostle Paul began a church in Philippi with a woman (Lydia) who was the first to believe.

As I already mentioned, the Bible tells us that God does not show partiality (Rom. 2:11). He doesn't play favorites. We are all equal in Christ. Unfortunately, throughout history, that level of equality has wavered depending on the culture and the country.

So I wonder, what more might Miriam have wanted? What could have caused her to complain against her brother with words that make her sound like she is defending herself? Somehow her attitude caused God to step in and show her that Moses was not in the wrong.

Have you ever struggled with jealousy? How easily do you complain? I might feel jealous when I long for something that God holds back from me yet gives to someone else. But more often, I find it far too easy to complain. Can you relate?

Do you compare your life to others and find yours wanting? When things don't turn out the way you expected, how do you react?

Some people, like my husband, can take life in stride and accept whatever comes their way. If plans change, he is easygoing enough to just go with it. Me? I want to know the plan and follow it. But as I've been learning in my years on earth, each day really does have enough trouble of its own. And trouble will come. I might plan to write all day and end up sitting in a hospital room or find myself interrupted with things I could not possibly foresee. Those 3:00 a.m. calls can mess with a day's schedule.

Or maybe we miss something we really wanted to attend because our circumstances took us elsewhere. Sometimes the opposite is true, and we find ourselves bored and lonely and unable to do anything because of physical limitations.

We struggle with growing older too. And Miriam was definitely aging. So perhaps she wasn't so much jealous as she was just weary. Weariness can lead us to complain, can't it?

We will never know the exact nature of the complaint against Moses's Cushite wife. But we do know Aaron and Miriam had a problem with her.

Have you ever found such struggles brewing in your family? Has there been a time when you competed with a sibling and perhaps felt less favored and wanted to tell them so? Or maybe you felt your parents didn't love you as much as your little sister or your older brother. Maybe you just don't like the choices your siblings are making.

This little passage of Scripture can cause all manner of speculation—everything from subtle jealousy to discontent to anger to hurt to feeling displaced. But we do need to guard our hearts against all of these possible scenarios in our own lives.

When we look at how the apostle Paul describes love in 1 Corinthians 13:4–5, we see that it "is very patient and kind, never jealous or envious, never boastful or proud, never haughty or selfish or rude. Love does not demand its own way. It is not irritable or touchy. It does not hold grudges and will hardly even notice when others do it wrong" (TLB).

If we are in relationship with people, there is going to be conflict. Guaranteed. Sometimes we do need to confront situations. But as Miriam found out, we had best be sure that we do so with the right motives and for the right reasons. If we confront out of anything but love, we run a great risk. We can make things worse for everyone.

## Imagine with Me

When the dreams began, I didn't know what to make of them. The images confused me sometimes but were clearer at other times. I saw the people in them, saw what they were doing, but I could not always understand what the dream meant. I did not realize the first time that God had singled me out to speak to me as He would a prophet. A sense of elation filled me that He would consider me worthy of such a privilege. I walked around in a daze for some time.

When the events in the dreams actually came to pass . . . that's when I had the courage to mention them to Jephunneh. I am not sure he believed me at first, but then I learned to trust him with the dreams before they came to pass, so that when they did, he knew I spoke truth.

I have felt a kinship with our God because of the dreams, and even when they frighten me, I feel nothing but awe. Why should our powerful God speak to me, a woman? And yet He does, over and over again.

Aaron hears His voice as well, though he hears God's word in visions more than dreams. Both of us wonder if Moses has had the same experience, especially when he lived in far-off Midian.

But here in the wilderness where we have wandered far longer than anyone expected, we have watched Moses spend more time with God—alone on the mountain or in the tabernacle. Both Aaron and I no longer hear from Him as we once did.

I ache with missing Him sometimes. And when Moses's face glows with the brightness of God's glory, I find my heart yearning to meet with God face-to-face as one does a friend. That's what Moses has—or seems to have. And I struggle with feelings I know I should not feel.

I walk over craggy paths as I meander through the tents, not headed in any particular direction. I just grow so weary of the tent, of the same food, of wandering. I never say so though. Moses does not need an uprising against him. People have already complained about the manna and missing the variety of food in Egypt. I do not miss Egypt.

My feet turn of their own accord toward Moses's tent in the Levite encampment. I spot his new wife sitting on the ground, spinning wool newly shorn. She is darker than we are. She is not of Jewish blood. And *I* used to fear I was wrong to marry a Judahite. How could Moses bring this woman into his tent with Zipporah barely in the grave? It's not like he is young and needs a wife to bear him sons.

I nod and greet her as I pass, but I do not linger. I should. I should welcome her into our family, but the whole situation doesn't seem right. She joined us out of Egypt, so she has seen the miracles, the devastation of that land. That doesn't mean Moses had to marry her after Zipporah died. My jaw clenches of its own accord.

*Would you have preferred he remain alone? Or did you want to be the one to meet his companionship needs?*

The words accuse me, and I turn back toward my tent, disgusted with myself. How selfish can I be? Surely the woman has qualities that I can learn to love. But after months of trying to feel right about their relationship, I simply can't.

I seek Aaron out, and he agrees. "Hasn't God spoken to us as well?" I ask. "How can Moses be so sure God wanted him to marry her?"

"She isn't one of us. As our head leader, he should have married within our clan, our tribe. Why hasn't God reprimanded him?" Aaron's white brows are furrowed, the lines along his forehead deep.

I tuck a wispy strand of hair beneath my scarf. "Perhaps we should talk to him."

But before we can act, as if out of a windstorm the voice of God calls to us. We are summoned to the tabernacle. A shiver works through me. What can this mean? Had God heard our complaints?

I walk beside Aaron, my feet weighted, dread filling me. I cannot see what is coming. If I had suspected that God would defend my brother . . . I would have taken a far different course.

## From Complaints to Humility

We are prone to complain against other people. I think we like to compare ourselves to others, don't we? And yet Jesus tells us not to think about another's future but to simply follow Him for our own lives.

Even Peter in the New Testament had a penchant for wanting to know what God's plans were for his friend John, instead of accepting what God had planned for him alone. Jesus had told Peter, "If it is my will that he [John] remain until I come, what is that to you? You follow me!" (John 21:22).

This incident reminds me of a time when I sensed Jesus' words applying to my situation. I was sitting in a Sunday school class at church and a friend was sitting nearby. I knew she and her husband were attempting to get pregnant. I had recently miscarried and longed to have a baby. Somehow, because I'd suffered, I couldn't bear the thought of her having a baby before I did. (Competition, anyone?) And in that moment, I heard these words in my heart: *If I want her to have ten children, what is that to you? You follow Me.*

By the way, that friend didn't have ten children. She had one. I had three, but by then there was no longer a competition in my heart. I was sufficiently convicted that Jesus mattered more than what I wanted. And what His plans are for others is none of my business.

I think Miriam needed to learn that too.

Miriam, who once sang songs of praise at the Israelites' deliverance from Egypt, ended up growing old and developed a comparative, complaining spirit. Perhaps some of that shift in her attitude came from the changes in her roles in her family and Israel. Where once she had held responsibility and positive leadership, as time passed, something changed. Did jealousy usurp her joy? Or did something else happen to make her complain about the way life had gone?

The Bible does not give us her motives. We can guess that she didn't have the highest regard for her new sister-in-law. And given her defensiveness regarding leadership and God's call on her life, I wonder if she might have grown jealous of Moses's relationship with God or of his role as the main leader of a people she probably knew better than he did. Somewhere along the way, she gave in to the temptation to complain against her brother, and her words caught God's attention. And He did not like hearing her complain against His servant Moses, whom the Bible says was the most humble, or meek, man, more than all of the people on earth (Num. 12:3).

When you look at God's relationship with Israel at this time, His anger seems to have been most aroused when the people complained. And the longer they wandered, and even after they inhabited the Promised Land, the longer they continued to complain, disobey, and distrust God, provoking Him to wrath. Does that convict you? It does me.

I don't see complaining as the same as crying out to God for help. When the Israelites were slaves in Egypt, God saw their misery and heard their cries, and He answered them with a great deliverance.

However, as I've studied the books surrounding Miriam's life, or even just done a devotional read-through of the first few books of the Bible, I've seen a pattern. The people of Israel complained a lot, which is really saying, "I don't trust You, Lord."

The Israelites couldn't find water after three days of searching, and when they did, it was bitter—in other words, undrinkable. So they complained to Moses. God told Moses how to freshen the water.

The people grew hungry, and instead of praying, they complained to Moses again. God gave them manna, or bread from heaven. They got sick of the manna and complained again, so God sent them quail.

The spies sent to Canaan, who were supposed to encourage the people to take the Promised Land as God intended, came back instead with a lot of negativity. Rather than rousing the people to move forward and follow God's lead, all but two of them told tales of giants in the land who were too big for them to overcome, which made the whole nation afraid. People grew whiny again, making God angry over their lack of trust. So they faced the unhappy consequence of wandering in the wilderness for forty years.

If Miriam didn't like Moses's choice of a wife, she could have talked it over with her husband (if she had one) or with Aaron's wife, and she could have asked God to help her understand why what Moses chose to do was okay. Seems like before complaining, she should have noticed the pattern that complaint equals consequences from God. But obviously, she didn't. Isn't it the same for us? It is easy to forget that God is listening to what we say. If He doesn't like what He hears, He may let us know that. If not now, then someday, when we will give an account to Him for our words.

Miriam had to face the consequences of her grumbling. She was stricken with a case of leprosy for seven days and forced to live outside the camp (Num. 12:10–15).

We might ask, Why such a harsh punishment? After all, it was a simple complaint. But I think we underestimate how God views our complaining spirits. We are telling Him that we know better. We don't think He's gotten things right. We don't trust Him with our future or our present. To complain against our circumstances, a fellow human being, or even God Himself (um, yeah, I've done all of those) is an affront to Him.

I sense that may be why Miriam suffered God's discipline. It wasn't that God stopped loving her. But He wanted her to realize that He is God. She was not. He chose Moses to lead. He chose her to lead in a different capacity. Maybe because leaders are held to a higher standard, God couldn't allow her words to go unnoticed.

It is a testament to Moses's humility and love for his sister that he begged God to heal her. Some siblings might not have been so gracious, given the complaint against them. Moses was. And yet, even Moses didn't have an "in" with God to stop Him from disciplining His child. Hebrews 12:6 tells us that God disciplines those He loves, and He showed that love by teaching Miriam to respect Him.

I suspect that Miriam came away chastised and humble. We don't hear of her again until her death, so we can't know how she felt. But if God put me through something like that, I think I'd learn a little humility. Perhaps I would even make an attempt to turn my complaint into acceptance.

Do you do that? Have you ever taken your jealous or complaining feelings and given them to God, asking Him to help you accept the blessings He's given you, even if they aren't the blessings you wanted?

God uses the things we would rather complain about to bring about change in us. He wants to make His children like His Son, Jesus. That may sound like God wants all His children to look alike, but that's not the case. He doesn't want clones of Christ. He wants His image bearers to actually bear the mark of His image in their character.

Do I love as Jesus did? To the point of being willing to sacrifice all for the sake of a loved one?

Do I have Jesus' patience? To the point where I am willing to wait on God even if He takes years to answer my prayers?

Do I have Jesus' compassion? To the point where I am willing to lay aside what I want to do in order to comfort someone else who needs me right then?

Do I have Jesus' perseverance? To the point where when trials hit hard, I can stand up under them by God's grace?

When God graciously uses other people to bless us, do we allow Him to use us to touch other people in the same way? Do we thank people for what they've done for us? Do we turn irritable attitudes on their heads, and instead of complaining about what we don't have, we thank God for what we do?

Most of the time things could be a lot worse in our lives. But I sense so much entitlement in our thinking today that it feels like we've lost the desire to pray and have forgotten the art of gratitude.

If the Israelites had not complained so many times, showing their lack of trust in God to lead them, I can bet they would not have wandered in the wilderness for forty years.

Are you wandering in a wilderness of your own right now? I am. Or at least it feels like I am—on and off. I've been here a long time, but I sense that God is finally getting my attention enough to pull me out of it. I'm growing stronger in my faith, and the complaints are fewer, the gratitude more often, the praise real.

Maybe I'm beginning to carry just a bit of the character of Jesus. I hope so. How about you?

## Ponder This

Life isn't going to go the way we expect it to. No one who lives on this planet gets everything they want. Even Jesus laid aside the right to dictate a perfect life for Himself here in order to prepare a place for us with Him in eternity that will be far beyond anything we could possibly ask for or imagine.

We are going to feel both good and bad emotions, deal with good and bad people, struggle with circumstances that don't go the way we expected, and even find joy in something that surprises us out of the blue. Whatever we face, we can take that circumstance or emotion and find the good in it. We can thank God even in the midst of trials. Maybe we aren't going to thank Him *for* the trial, but we can thank Him *in* it. He is working things for our good if we love Him. And loving Him takes a lifetime to truly learn.

Remember this:

> For I am sure that neither death nor life, nor angels nor rulers, nor things present nor things to come, nor powers, nor height nor depth, nor anything else in all creation, will be able to separate us from the love of God in Christ Jesus our Lord. (Rom. 8:38–39)

God loves you. If you have put your trust in Jesus Christ and believed what God says about Him, you belong to God, not to this world. You are here to fulfill the things God planned in advance for you to do, and to allow God our Father to shape you into the image of the Lord Jesus Christ.

Oftentimes the journey of growing to become like Christ —or, as in Miriam's case, to be obedient to God—is not easy. It is more likely the hardest thing we will ever do. But it is worth every step along the way.

## TAKING IT FURTHER

1. Do you think Miriam and Aaron should have been equal partners with Moses in leading Israel? Can you relate to why Miriam might have grown jealous of her brother's favor with God? Why or why not?

2. Have you ever compared your situation in life to someone else's? How has that comparison made you feel? What might you do differently the next time you are tempted to feel jealous, complain, or compare yourself to someone who seems to live an easier or better life than you?

3. What are some positive things you can do to grow closer to God? Name three things you can begin to do right now that will make God more real to you and start you on a path toward a greater intimacy with the Creator who loves you.

# Daring to Trust What You Cannot See

*(Based on Joshua 2—6)*

## If I Were Rahab

Something has shifted in the atmosphere here, as though whatever light that once came from the sun to heat the homes of Jericho has changed. While it still shines, the warmth is gone, replaced by cold fear.

The darkness of this place has been part of my life longer than I can remember, ever since my husband was sold to pay for his debts and I was sold to Dabir and a life I would not have chosen. Wealthy men have paid for time with me for too long, but now they come to tell me what keeps them awake at night. Terror fills them, from the least to the greatest. I see it in the marketplace, in my neighbors and servants, even in my family.

I did not expect to find it coming from the palace.

"Have you not seen them, Rahab?" the prince asked the last time he came to me. "They are like a horde of locusts on the plains."

I twisted a strand of hair through my fingers. "Do you mean the Hebrews? They have wandered the wilderness for forty years. What is there to fear of them behind our stout walls?"

The prince stared at me and shook his head. "I would have expected you to be more aware, with all of the men who come bearing tales to you."

I laughed. "They are usually interested in more than talking." I did not tell him how much I had learned from those who visit my door.

He leaned on one elbow and ran his fingers up my arm. "Nevertheless, they are not to be taken lightly. Even my father huddles in the palace and confers with his generals. They are desperate to find out all they can of these people who walked through the Red Sea and destroyed the Egyptian army, not to mention the more recent victories over the kings Og and Sihon on the other side of the Jordan. Now they are at our door. Do you not find that troublesome?"

I studied this man who had done so much for and against me throughout my lifetime. He could show such mercy and yet, when pushed, could also be cruel. If not for him, my husband might still be with me, but my husband was a fool. The prince's patience could not last forever. And he had spared me much. Still, I did not trust him. I trusted no one in this city.

I weighed my words carefully, as I always did when speaking to men of power. "I think the men in this city worry more than they should. Yes, the Hebrews have been mighty warriors a few times. But it has taken them over forty years to move from Egypt to Canaan. Why would a journey that should have taken perhaps two weeks take so much longer?"

"They say their god had something to do with that."

"They say their god gave them the victories over Egypt and Og and Sihon too. Is it their god our king fears? Are not our gods strong enough to protect us?" I was goading him, but he did not see it. I have learned how to get information without giving it in return. One never knows when she will need to use someone's words to save her own life. I know this too well.

But now, the weight of the prince's fear stays with me, and I cannot escape the feeling that he is right. I look from my window to the plains beyond. The Hebrews are too many to count, and the more I learn of their history from other men who visit, the more I respect them and their God.

Perhaps that is why I was not surprised when two of their spies came to me as darkness fell upon Jericho. Or that the king had watched my house and knew they had come.

I let out a breath and look down at the scarlet cord hanging from my window. My gaze shifts to the hills where I sent the spies to escape the guards who pursue them even now. Had they made it away in time? I strain my eyes, but I cannot see far enough to notice moving objects in the darkness. Not even an owl hoots or a bird shows its silhouette in the light of the moon.

The spies promised to protect anyone in my house. Tomorrow I will try to convince my family to live with me. Will they come? My father can be stubborn, and I have no certainty that I will be able to convince them without telling them what I know. And I cannot tell. I promised the spies I would keep their secret.

I glance heavenward then, arms leaning against the sill of the window. *Do You see me? Are You real?* I want to believe in the Hebrew God. My people fear Him, but their fear carries no faith. They are terrified. I fear Him with a healthy sense of awe. I respect Him. And I believe the tales and the spies. I believe their God will take our city and kill our citizens. Hadn't He promised them this land?

And yet, I must admit it is hard to trust the stories when you cannot see the God who brought them about. Though the parting of the Red Sea and the humiliation of Egypt happened long before my birth, I have heard of every plague, down to the death of the firstborns, and how the entire Egyptian army drowned in the sea when they tried to chase after the Hebrews. Their God is more powerful than the gods of Egypt. He is more powerful than the gods of the kingdoms of Sihon and Og, so He is certainly more powerful than the gods my people worship.

It isn't that I don't believe. It's that I don't know. I haven't seen. I have met the spies and heard their promises to me. I know the Hebrews are coming soon, and I have bargained to keep my family alive. But I do not know for certain that they will be spared.

I suppose I have faith mixed with doubt. Isn't that what trust in anything comes down to? Faith in what we cannot see? It would not be faith if we could see it.

I look once more at the scarlet cord hanging from my window. The symbol the Hebrews had told me to put there to single my home out from the rest so they would know which one to spare. I tug on the end that is securely tied to my bedpost beneath the heavy curtains. After all of the knots I have tied in it, there is no chance it will come loose, and I have hidden it well so no one will notice it from inside the house. Unless our men go outside the protection of our walls and look up, I am safe.

I draw in a shaky breath. I will be safe with the Hebrews, won't I? I *can* trust their God. Somehow I know I can, even though I cannot see Him. In any case, I have made my choice. I would trust my life and that of my family into the care of the Hebrews and their God rather than in the life I now know and hate, and the people I know and dare not trust.

I just hope I am not trading the familiar, which feels safe, for an unfamiliar risk that could prove very foolish. I do not want to regret my choice.

## What We Know

In Rahab's time, most people put their faith in physical objects and called them gods. They would carve an image of a person or animal or a combination of both and cover it with gold or silver or bronze. Houses might have statues of these images, or people might have made Asherah poles, which somehow represented their gods. In King David's day, the Philistines worshiped Dagon, a god that is said to have been half fish, half man. The Canaanites worshiped Molech, a bronze god with arms to hold a living child meant to be devoured in the flames of its belly.

Other cultures of Rahab's day worshiped the sun (Egypt called it Ra), the moon (Mesopotamia and other places called it Sin), and the stars. If you study the ancient world, you'll find all sorts of gods and goddesses, even before the time of the legendary gods of the Greeks.

The worship of things other than our one Creator has been around since the devil wanted to *be* God and have the glory that belongs to God alone be his. And he's been trying to get us to worship him or do his bidding ever since.

I know that might sound strange because devil or Satan worship is so diabolical and evil. But in the New Testament, we learn that meat offered to idols was really meat offered to demons because behind every idol stood a demon (1 Cor. 10:19–21). So when God told the Israelites to wipe out the Canaanites and destroy their gods lest those gods become a snare to them, He was essentially getting rid of the demon control of that land.

God has always held power over the demonic world, and He has proven it over and over again in Scripture and in our world today. He proved His power most thoroughly in the resurrection of Jesus Christ from death, a feat none of us can or could do no matter how much we might want to.

In some cultures today, the devil—or the enemy, as I prefer to call him—still deceives people into the worship of actual physical idols. In fact, there are cultures, even nations, in our world whose people are held captive by demonic forces, and their cruelty and oppression are very real. In the United States, I think we often underestimate the power the enemy holds over these people, because here that power comes to us in far more subtle ways.

But we must not be fooled. Jesus said the enemy comes to steal, kill, and destroy (John 10:10), and he is still trying his level best to do just that. Never underestimate the power of false gods even in our neighborhoods and multicultural belief systems. Jesus is greater, but the devil is stronger than we are without Jesus. When we come against the enemy in prayer, he will work to defeat those prayers. We pray in the power of the Holy Spirit and wear the armor of God so we can war against the unseen powers that are against us. We forgive as we've been forgiven, and we submit to God so the devil will flee from us. God wants us to be wise enough to be aware of the devil's schemes, as the apostle Paul said (2 Cor. 2:11; Eph. 6:11).

In our Western culture, idolatry is more temptingly indirect than it was in days gone by. I see it on television, in movies, on social media, even on the news. It's not hard to find our new and indistinct idols. We worship whatever controls us. That might be an addiction to any number of practices or substances or even to power. Some have taken to acknowledging the created universe in place of the God who created it, as though the universe in itself has power of some sort.

Self-worship is another false god today. *Do what feels good to you . . . Whatever makes you happy . . . You deserve it . . . Don't let anyone tell you what to do . . . Be autonomous . . .* You've heard it, haven't you?

Just a walk through a local department store shows children's clothing emblazoned with words like "I can do anything" and "I can conquer the world." Really? That may sound innocent, but . . . I wonder.

Alexander the Great thought he could conquer the world. Roman emperors pushed their boundaries until they controlled a powerful empire. The Persian king Xerxes conquered a lot of his world. Hitler wanted world domination. But most of the people in these positions were self-serving despots. Is that really the message we want to give our boys and girls?

I used to believe we *could* do anything if we wanted to badly enough. We think we can have it all until we put something off so long we truly *can't* have what we want.

As we grow a little older and meet more people, we realize maybe we can't do everything—or anything—we want to do. We all have limitations. Athletic hopefuls get seriously injured and never walk again. Strange diseases hit a child and keep the doctors scratching their heads because they simply can't find a solution. Super intelligent people fall on hard times, lose hope, and end up homeless or addicted to some substance.

When we allow ourselves to put other things in place of God's spot in our hearts and our lives, we're never going to find true satisfaction.

Even Christians, if we're not careful, can fall into the same thinking. We take the verse "Love your neighbor as yourself" (Mark 12:31) as an excuse for self-focus, self-love, self-pursuit, and doing what feels right in our own eyes. But I think we fail to look at that verse the way Jesus intended it. We misread Scripture to feed our own idols.

Jesus didn't say love yourself so you can love your neighbor. He said love your neighbor as yourself because we already love ourselves enough. I realize that some of us have had our self-esteem beaten down and we don't love ourselves at all. I understand that feeling—I've been there.

But the answer isn't to try to find some new way to love ourselves so we feel better. The answer is to love God more because He will show us just how much He already loves us. When we truly comprehend how great the Father's love is for us, the love He has lavished upon us, we don't have to allow those beat-up feelings any power over us. God loves us! His heart beats for ours. We are His special possession.

So we don't have to twist those verses to love ourselves in order to love our neighbor. Jesus taught His disciples to deny themselves, take up their cross, and follow Him (Matt. 16:24). He promised suffering and persecution for His followers (2 Tim. 3:12). He called the road narrow and said few would find it (Matt. 7:14). He said that loving meant patience with others, sacrifice, believing the best (1 Cor. 13), and forgiving 490-plus times a day if need be (Matt. 18:21–22).

Love has become as twisted in our culture as it was to Rahab when she lived a life of prostitution. Sometimes we

are so focused on us and thinking the worst about ourselves that we end up being even more self-centered than
we realize.

(Side note: If you truly feel that you are not worth loving
or you honestly hate yourself, I am not suggesting that I have
all of the answers. Trained counselors might be necessary to
help you get past feelings of hating yourself. But sometimes
we are just too self-focused.)

I'll give you an example. When I was in my early twenties,
I had a conscience that often condemned me. I'm an introvert,
but an anxious one who often talks too much when I'm nervous. That nervous chatter can lead to self-condemnation. If
I was at a gathering of people and talked too much, I would
go home and rehash in my mind everything I'd said. I would
go back and apologize to people I feared I had offended. But
you know what? Ninety-nine percent of the time those people
didn't remember the words or incidents and never thought
about them again. Not like I did. I would beat myself up when
I hadn't done anything wrong.

Now I see it not only as nerves but also as oversensitivity.
And I realize that when I'm oversensitive, I'm thinking too
much about me.

Can you relate? You say "Hi" to someone, and if they don't
respond you might feel hurt. But maybe they didn't hear you.
Maybe they were focused on something they had to do. They
weren't shunning you. They might have brushed past you because they couldn't remember your name and didn't want to
feel embarrassed. Or they were late for a meeting or weren't
feeling well. There are so many different scenarios.

I've learned to give people the benefit of the doubt and cut
them some slack. And when I can do that for others, I can do
that for myself as well.

Like Rahab, we need to learn to trust in what we cannot see, not in the false gods that we can see. Sometimes that means trusting God for the very first time. Or perhaps we've lost that initial trust and need to find it again. When we can trust the God we cannot see, He makes it easier to trust our fellow human beings. That's a lesson Rahab risked her life to learn.

## Imagine with Me

The breeze kisses my face as I walk from the tent I now share with my husband, Salmon, to Joshua's tent, where Joshua's wife and I agreed to make food for the leaders who will soon descend on the men. My hand moves of its own accord to the bulge beneath my robe. The babe kicks, a healthy though tiny blow against my belly. I can't help the joy that bubbles within me every time I feel it.

That day in Jericho, which lies in burned ruins across the plain now, I could never have imagined that life would bring me here. My faith in the Hebrew God, *my* God, was not misplaced. Not only has He spared my life, He has also removed the shame of my former life. It is as though who I was before this moment never existed—a distant memory that no longer brings anger or pain.

I wave to several women at the doors of their tents as I walk toward Eliana's home. Salmon meets me at the door. He had come earlier to speak to Joshua alone. He kisses my cheek.

"You look beautiful today, as always." His smile warms me to my toes, and I stare at them, heat creeping up my neck at the way he looks at me. He touches my chin and lifts my gaze to his. "Are you shying away from a compliment from your husband?"

I smile wide. "You know . . . before . . . men would say that to me because they wanted something from me. But with you, with your people—"

"Our people," he interrupts me.

"Our people." I nod. "I believe that when you say such things you truly mean them. I know you love me. I even think that somehow God loves me." I cradle the babe in both hands. "After everything else, He's given us this child. He's blessed me—an undeserving outcast. Yet because I believed Him and trusted Him to protect me . . . well, He gave me so much more."

Salmon pulls me close. "He always does, my love. What other nation on earth can say they have a God who sought them out and called them His own? What other nation has a God who loves them and only asks for our love in return?"

"None I have ever heard of. The gods of Jericho were not like that. Neither were the gods of the nations around us." I had known it back then, and I know it stronger now, deep in my bones.

"And none ever can or will, because there is no other God." He leans back and kisses my forehead. "I am very grateful that He brought you into my life." He touches the babe and is rewarded with another kick. He laughs, and I love the sound of it. Never have I loved a man as I do Salmon. Never has a man been so selfless as he.

"I'd best let you get inside to help Eliana. She is waiting for you." He kisses me again, right there in front of Joshua's tent. The joy rises higher. Salmon is not ashamed to call me his. Just as God is not ashamed to be called my God.

I'm not sure I will ever get over the wonder of it all.

## From Fragile Trust to Certainty

Rahab is commended in the book of Hebrews as a woman of faith. "By faith Rahab the prostitute did not perish with those who were disobedient, because she had given a friendly welcome to the spies" (11:31). In James 2:25, her faith is linked to these works of saving the spies. Her faith was visible, but it also came with her exacting a promise from the spies to spare her family (Josh. 2:8–14). She took a risk to trust these men she did not know, and her words in Joshua base that faith on what she had heard of the Lord their God.

We can't know how weak or strong her faith was in that moment. I explored her story in more depth in *The Crimson Cord: Rahab's Story*. But not much is told of her in Scripture except this incident and one other significant piece of information that God wanted us to know about her. She married a man named Salmon, who became the father of Boaz. Boaz was the father of Obed by Ruth, who was also a foreigner grafted into the line of Israel. Obed was the father of Jesse, who was the father of King David. If you read the genealogy in Matthew 1, you see that Jesus the Messiah came from this line of David.

Rahab's faith landed her in the lineage of grace—the line of Christ.

Can you imagine how she might have felt as her faith grew from that tentative, risky trust to certainty that God and Israel had accepted her? She became one of their people by faith.

Sometimes our faith in Christ starts strong. Sometimes it begins with a tiny seed that grows over time. My dad was four years old when he walked a sawdust trail at a tent revival meeting, and his faith stuck. Did he ever doubt? I don't know. He was human, so probably a time or two. But when one of our kids came to faith in Jesus Christ at age four, I asked my dad, "Is four too young?" He said, "I was four." And outside of my husband, I don't know another man I would call more faithful to the Lord than my dad.

My husband was in his twenties when he came to faith. But it also stuck. He never doubted God after that. He'd seen too many reasons to believe, and as we have grown in our walk with God, his faith has only grown stronger, deeper. I see it in him. And I see it in me. Even when we face trials and suffering and heartache and any number of struggles we're going to face in this life, his faith and hope remain strong, like my dad's.

They say certain diseases can rob our memories. Things like Alzheimer's (a horrible disease!), dementia, short-term memory loss, and even tumors or concussions can affect the memory portion of our brains. Not to mention aging. I forget things too. It drives me crazy when I walk into a room to get something and then forget what I went there to get! I have to turn around, walk back the way I came, and then I remember.

You can hear what I'm saying, can't you? There wouldn't be a "Find My Phone" feature on cell phones if we didn't lose or forget things.

My dad had trouble with his memory as he aged. He always knew me though—except once. But it didn't take long for him to remember. Good thing too, because I was about to burst into tears at his sudden confusion.

After he'd spent a few years of his life in a nursing home, we found out he was dying. There was nothing they could do in his condition except call in hospice (which is great, by the way). As I watched him grow weaker, I spent as much time with him as I could. We told him he only had a few months left on earth. One day one of the workers told me that he had said he was "going to be with my Father soon."

That faith of a four-year-old? He never forgot it, or his God. He might have almost forgotten his daughter for a brief moment, but he did not forget his Father in heaven. He wasn't afraid to go there because he'd spent his life growing that faith from fragile trust to adamant certainty. Years of reading his

Bible cover to cover had made him so familiar with his God that not even memory loss could take that from him.

I have to admit, I'm pretty happy about that. I'm still proud of my dad in an admiring sort of way. Not because he was perfect or did everything right. Not because he never suffered hardship or never let stress get the better of him sometimes. But when he faced life's struggles, he knew where to turn. He always came back to trust in the Lord.

I wasn't always in a good place when I was a kid. The stress my dad and mom dealt with trickled onto me sometimes. If you read my previous nonfiction book, *When Life Doesn't Match Your Dreams*, then you know some of my story. It wasn't always happy.

It's amazing what God can teach you as you write a book (and read a ton of them in preparation for writing it). It's amazing what God can teach you through His Word, through trials, through grace. I think that maybe, just maybe, I'm starting to learn some of what my dad learned.

Life might not always go the way we'd like it to. Suffering happens to all of us in one way or another. No family is perfect. No relationship is without challenges. No country has discovered utopia. No religion has answers to all of our questions in this life.

Even those of us who believe in Jesus Christ will struggle to understand the "why" questions of life. Jesus promised that if His followers wanted to live godly lives, they would suffer persecution (2 Tim. 3:12). It's not my favorite part of Scripture, but it's true.

One thing God is teaching me about trust is that there is no other way to live. If I believe God is sovereign, in control of all things, then I also know that where I am right now in my life is where He has placed me.

Maybe it's a wonderful place, like David once said: "The boundary lines have fallen for me in pleasant places; surely I have a delightful inheritance" (Ps. 16:6 NIV). Or maybe it's in the bottom of a pit where, like Joseph, we have landed against our will. Joseph waited twenty-two years to be reconciled with the brothers who betrayed him. Maybe it's waiting on a promise God gave us, like Sarah hoping for a child and waiting twenty-five years to hold that baby in her arms. Maybe it's longing for something we don't know if we will ever have, like Hannah when she prayed for a child. She didn't know for certain until she prayed like never before. When Eli blessed her, I think she knew. God had heard her prayer.

Just like God heard Rahab and commended her throughout history. Just like God hears you and me when we come to Him, no matter our circumstances, with trusting hearts.

## Ponder This

Remember, Rahab didn't have much to go on when she welcomed the spies and decided to trust their God. She had heard stories of their God's actions against other nations, but she had no personal interaction with or knowledge of Him herself.

Sometimes, when it comes to faith, we don't have much more understanding or knowledge than Rahab did. We may hear stories of what Jesus did for others, yet that faith cannot become ours secondhand. Ultimately, faith in what Jesus did for us and offers to us must become personal and intimate between Him and us alone. We can't rely on another's faith or even stand strong on a weak faith.

Rahab's faith started out weak, but it became strong. That's the kind of faith we need if we're going to live fully alive in a broken, troubled, and evil world.

Finally, be strong in the Lord and in his mighty power. Put on the full armor of God, so that you can take your stand against the devil's schemes. For our struggle is not against flesh and blood, but against the rulers, against the authorities, against the powers of this dark world and against the spiritual forces of evil in the heavenly realms. Therefore put on the full armor of God, so that when the day of evil comes, you may be able to stand your ground, and after you have done everything, to stand. (Eph. 6:10–13 NIV)

We need not trust in man-made idols or man-made ideologies or even in ourselves—not when we have a Creator who sovereignly holds the world in His hands. And like no other god could, He loves us and will give us the grace to trust Him no matter what life brings.

## TAKING IT FURTHER

1. Do you think Rahab had enough information to trust two spies over her own people? If you stood in her shoes, do you think you could have taken such a risk to trust a people and a God you did not know? Why or why not?

2. Have you come to a place where you trust God with your life, your future, your soul? How might sharing your faith strengthen it?

3. If you had to put your faith on a scale between fragile and strong, where would it land? Does the thought of risking all for Christ scare you? Is living a godly life worth the risk to you? Why or why not?

# Deborah

## Dealing with God's Call

*(Based on Judges 4–5)*

### If I Were Deborah

I should be used to the dreams by now, but I wake with a start just the same. What are these strange things I see? All of Israel gathered to fight Sisera and his men? We are weak, disjointed tribes with no leader. Even our general, Barak, is not strong enough against the might of Sisera.

The dreams scare me, but the visions are worse. Lappidoth tells me that I fall into a trance, and I believe him, for I cannot hear or see what is going on around me. The battle is too real, and the people coming to me for help often overwhelm me. I know from what little we have of the law that God speaks to prophets in visions and dreams, but I am no prophet. Or prophetess.

Am I?

I will admit I struggle with this. My husband tells me that God has called me to lead. And when the first people began to show up at our door asking me to judge between them, I didn't know quite what to do. Eventually, I moved to sit beneath a large palm tree in the center of our small walled village. But then men from surrounding tribes heard of me and came. Our guards have become extra vigilant to keep us from becoming too well known. We are a small community and hidden from Sisera's men. I pray it stays that way, though the dreams tell me we will face him one day.

I do not look forward to that day.

The truth, when I face it, is that it is not easy to be called by God. So far all of the dreams and visions have come true. Therefore, I have to believe my husband is right. God has a reason for choosing me to act as judge in Israel. Lappidoth helps me, as he is a scribe by trade, but it seems as though God Himself gives me understanding of the law when I'm faced with a judgment that appears too difficult.

Sometimes I wish He had chosen someone else. Who am I to lead men? Who am I to tell other people what to do? I am a mother, a grandmother. I would be happy to do the work those jobs require without adding this one. But that is not God's plan for me.

A commotion at the gate draws my attention, and I see Barak, the one man who continues to try to fight against our enemies, walking toward me, his men in tow. It is time. God has given me a word to give to this man, and yet I do not know if he is ready to hear it.

*Tell Barak that God has said, "The Lord, the God of Israel, commands you: 'Go, take with you ten thousand men of Naphtali and Zebulun, and lead them up to Mount Tabor. I will lead*

*Sisera, the commander of Jabin's army, with his chariots and his troops to the Kishon River and give him into your hands.'"*

Barak stands before me now, and the words ring in my ears.

"You sent for me?" he asks, fire in his eyes. Perhaps he is more ready than I think.

"The Lord has sent for you." I hold his steady gaze and repeat the words God has given to me.

Barak listens, but with each word from my mouth, the fire in his gaze dampens a little more, replaced by fear. He is silent for a lengthy moment.

"If you go with me, I will go, but if you don't go with me, I won't go." He crosses his arms as though warding off a chill . . . or possibly warding off my words. Is he afraid to obey our God without my help? He has seen much horror from Sisera and his men. I have no doubt it is that horror that holds him back now.

"Certainly I will go with you," I tell him. "But because of the course you are taking, the honor will not be yours, for the Lord will deliver Sisera into the hands of a woman." I know that woman will not be me, and I sincerely hope it will not be my daughter, whose fighting spirit worries me. But God's words in my heart cannot be clearer.

"It will be as you say," Barak says, seemingly satisfied. He releases a breath. "I will leave at dawn to assemble the troops at Kedesh. Can you join me that soon?"

"I can join you." I know God is not calling us to hesitate but to act. If I have learned anything in the years since God first put His call on my life, it is that when He gives a command, He means for it to be obeyed right away. Not when we feel like it, someday in the future.

I invite Barak and his men to stay in our home and prepare for our journey to Kedesh at dawn.

## What We Know

The Bible tells us very little about most of the judges who ruled for limited periods of time. Deborah is the only female judge Israel ever knew. She was also a prophetess and married to a man named Lappidoth. From her song, sung with Barak after their victory over Sisera, we can speculate that she was also a mother, for she calls herself a mother in Israel. She helped lead Israel alongside Barak in the biggest fight facing them—against a cruel king and his commander, Sisera. And her prophecy that a woman rather than Barak would kill Sisera came true.

While we do not know much about Deborah's personal life, which I imagined in my novel *The Prophetess: Deborah's Story*, we can apply some of what she lived through to our lives today.

Let's start with God's call on our lives. What do you think of when you think about a calling from God?

I grew up in a church that put emphasis on becoming a missionary or going into some other type of Christian service. To do such work was to do the work of God. There didn't seem to be any place for work outside of the local church that might also be considered a ministry or calling from God.

The trouble with this type of thinking is that it made some people feel as though they weren't really serving the Lord unless they were doing so at church. Now, I'm not trying to put down churches, because the church is Christ's body, and we all have unique gifts and callings. Paul was commissioned by God to preach the truth of Jesus' death and resurrection, just as Deborah was chosen by God to be a judge and prophetess in Israel.

Do you ever wonder how she felt about that? The Israelites were living in desperate times as an enemy king and his general raped and pillaged them every chance they got. People lived in hiding. Deborah's influence was known, but I don't know if it was known the whole length of Israel. However big it was, she took up the mantle God had given to her and did the work, whether she wanted to or not.

Other prophets didn't like being called by God to do His will. Consider Jonah, who ran from God's call. Elijah followed God faithfully, until he despaired even of life because of fear. Jeremiah is known as the "weeping prophet." He wasn't allowed to marry, and I rather doubt he enjoyed his call, especially when it landed him in a pit.

In our day, I think we may have to consider God's calling in a way we haven't before. Let me try to explain.

When I was growing up in that church, I feared that God was going to ask me to become a missionary to some place overseas, because those were the places missionaries went at the time. And I didn't want to go to any nation other than the one I knew.

I'm not exactly sure how I ended up knowing that overseas missions was not my calling. As I've matured in my walk with God, however, I think we can consider three things:

1. We can't put restrictions on what God wants to do.
2. God's call on our lives might not be our main goal.
3. God's call on our lives might be exactly what we
   desire.

I know those last two seem to contradict one another, but when we place our lives in God's hands, we aren't necessarily going to know right away where His calling will lead us.

And there is a difference between God's gifts and His call. There is also more than one type of calling from God.

Scripture tells us that God calls all people to believe in Him. We can't even come to Him without that first call. If we hear His call—and those who are seeking Him will hear Him—then it is up to us to respond to it. This is the beginning of a relationship with God, by believing in Jesus, the One whom the Father sent to be our Savior to reconcile us to Himself (1 John 4:13–15).

The second call of God is not the call of faith but the call of works. That might sound like I'm promoting a works-based faith, but I'm not. Rather, I'm reminding us that faith without works is dead (James 2:26). This call is not only for pastors and evangelists and church workers. It is universal for anyone who would be a disciple of Jesus Christ.

So what is the call? Jesus told His disciples, "I have been given all authority in heaven and on earth. Therefore, go and make disciples of all the nations, baptizing them in the name of the Father and the Son and the Holy Spirit. Teach these new disciples to obey all the commands I have given you. And be sure of this: I am with you always, even to the end of the age" (Matt. 28:18–20 NLT).

Every one of us is called to tell other people about Jesus. That's not a popular mission today. We have become a "tolerant" people, and that trickles down to accepting what anyone believes, no matter what that may be, as their truth. If they believe it, it is true for them. We are expected to accept everything as true. But if we take that to its logical conclusion, then nothing is true. If we do not have a truth that is absolutely true all of the time without end, then nothing is true because no truth will last. It will die with the person who believes it.

So bearing witness to the truth or attempting to make disciples of all nations as Jesus commanded His followers is tricky today. Many of us would rather remain silent than offend anyone. I know I often feel that way.

But if this is the calling given to every believer in Christ, then what do we do with it? Run away like Jonah? Rebel and do our own thing like Samson? Or obey God despite the consequences, like Jeremiah, Elijah, Moses, Abraham, Paul, and so many others listed in Hebrews' Hall of Faith (Heb. 11)?

This is where our calling and gifts can come together. God gave us gifts to build up people in the church—fellow believers— and we should use them to do that. But sometimes God calls us to use our gifts and talents to follow His call outside of the church.

Does that mean we have to go overseas to be a missionary? If God asks us to go, we should be willing. And that's the key Deborah must have learned. She had to be willing to listen to God and speak up when He told her to. Just as we need to do when God gives us such opportunities.

While we must be willing to obey God's call wherever that may lead, He often works through our desires. Turns out He never asked me to become a missionary to foreign lands. He asked me to use my gift of teaching to write stories that would point people to His Word. And those books have traveled to distant lands in a way I never could. But if the day comes when He asks me to stop using my gift in this way, I will.

He also put on my heart a desire to be a wife and a mom and then blessed me with a wonderful husband and three awesome sons. He gave me the desire to teach them about Jesus and to do my best to show them God Himself loves them—even more than their parents ever could, though parental love is strong. The gift of teaching was the same, just used in a different way.

Years ago, God also gave me a desire to co-teach a Bible study with a friend to a group of neighborhood women who didn't have the same Bible knowledge we had. The calling at that time was to study and teach, and I loved it.

All of these callings were the same—use the gift of teaching to tell others about Jesus; make disciples of every nation, be they many or few. When God calls us to follow Him and gives us gifts to use to complete the work He has given us (Eph. 2:10), we may find ourselves using them in different ways depending on the seasons of our lives.

God put the desire to tell people about Jesus in my heart at an early age. I was known as a Christian throughout school and shared my faith (taught what I knew) as early as fifth grade. People thought I was just spouting my parents' beliefs, but if that were true, I wouldn't have the same desire today. My faith is my own, and God's call hasn't changed. I just use it differently today than I did back then.

The same is true for all of us. The key is to be aware of what God has gifted us with and where He is leading us to use those gifts in each circumstance of our lives.

## Imagine with Me

Sisera's defeat surprises all of us. While I knew that a woman would kill him, I thought she would be a woman of Israel. But Jael is the wife of Heber the Kenite. I should know by now that God does not work in the ways I expect Him to.

But throughout our history, God has chosen men to lead our people, from Abraham to Moses and Joshua, who led us to the Promised Land. Even the judges who preceded me were men. Surely a man could have commanded a greater following than I have.

I pick up a drum and beat the goatskin covering with my right hand. The people have returned to the top of the hill after the victory, and Barak and I cannot help but give praise to our God. Who else could have given Israel such a great victory? Jael would not have had the chance to kill Sisera if not for God.

Words of praise flow from my mouth.

"Most blessed of women be Jael,
   the wife of Heber the Kenite,
   most blessed of tent-dwelling women.
He asked for water, and she gave him milk;
   in a bowl fit for nobles she brought him curdled
     milk.
Her hand reached for the tent peg,
   her right hand for the workman's hammer.
She struck Sisera, she crushed his head,
   she shattered and pierced his temple.
At her feet he sank, he fell;
   where he sank, there he fell—dead."

I glance at the crowd of mostly men, though Jael and her family have joined us. I smile her way. And then my gaze shifts heavenward as Barak picks up the rest of the song.

Adonai has been good to us, despite the sins of Israel that brought us to this place. We were a people with no king, and somewhere along the way our God was no longer looked to as our Lord and King.

When Moses led our people, God alone was worshiped. Joshua held the same authority as Moses, and people followed the Lord. My parents taught me this worship, but I have not seen many follow our Lord in my lifetime. For generations since Joshua's death, we have wandered from truth. And when we do, our enemies oppress us until we cry out to God to rescue us. In His grace, He always does, through the judges. I suppose I am one of them.

More will follow after me, and when I rest with my people, I wonder how long it will take for Israel to fall away from trusting and obeying God—again. I pray they will not. It hurts my heart to think that my grandchildren might face the terrors we have lived with for twenty years. Will we never learn that

God alone has the power to redeem us? Will we never learn that He deserves our trust, our praise?

The questions live with me many days after the battle. We are free now, and our people no longer live in hiding. But I am not young. How long will they live in this freedom? When will they stop thinking that what seems right to them, if it goes against the laws of our God, isn't?

I do not really want to know the answer to that question.

## From Hearing to Acting

Deborah lived in a terrible time. Sisera was the equivalent of a modern-day terrorist. He had weapons of war that far outweighed anything Israel possessed. He oppressed the people of Israel for twenty years, and God allowed it. Why? Because once the previous judge died, the people fell into doing what was right in their own eyes—worshiping other gods, pursuing whatever they wanted whether they were obeying the law of God or not. Trouble is, what seems right to us often isn't. As Solomon said in Proverbs 14:12, "There is a way that *seems* right to a man, but its end is the way to death" (emphasis mine).

Judges is a book that could find its way to the front pages of our most popular newspapers. History might change names and faces, but human nature does not improve with the passage of time. Whatever we want to believe about sin, our natures are bent on giving in to it. That's the whole point of Genesis. And without an understanding of Genesis, we miss an understanding of history. So we end up repeating it.

Deborah heard the call of God on her life in the middle of a frightening world. Stand up and speak for God to a people who had rejected Him? To a people who were suffering under horrible oppression? That took courage. Don't ever think that our maleness or femaleness makes a difference when it comes to whom God will use. Deborah was willing. Barak was not—not without Deborah. So while we remember Barak for his skills as a general and fighting man, we remember Deborah and Jael for their obedience and courage in the face of daunting odds. They acted differently from most women of their day.

All of us face obstacles to doing what God might want us to. Jesus often taught in parables, and He would end with this phrase: "He who has ears to hear, let him hear."

Later James, the brother of Jesus, wrote, "But prove yourselves doers of the word, and not merely hearers who delude themselves" (James 1:22 NASB). In other words, if we know the truth and we have given our hearts to Christ, then we have heard His words. But we still have a choice. Will we simply listen? Or will we act?

Deborah listened and acted. Barak listened and hesitantly acted. I'm not sure if God minds that we may be hesitant, but quick obedience to what we know is right and true and from Him garners a greater reward. As Deborah told Barak, "Because of the course you are taking, the honor will not be yours, for the LORD will deliver Sisera into the hands of a woman" (Judges 4:9 NIV). Barak still led his army to victory, and for his obedience he is listed in Hebrews' Hall of Faith, but he didn't get the honor for Sisera's personal defeat.

Deborah is a lesson in obedient trust for us today. She knew the call of God on her life, and she learned to listen and obey Him. We can't know if this was hard for her or if she found it easy to lead. We don't know if she questioned her ability or had a strong personality and found taking charge no big deal. But my guess is that because she was a woman in that culture, she had a few moments of second-guessing herself. I think we all do that at times, don't we?

I second-guess myself a lot. Sometimes I look back and think, *Could I have done that better?* I wish I'd said this instead of that. And with *every* book I write, my sweet husband and my critique partners and friends listen to me say how awful the book is . . . why did I ever think I could do this?

Until I can. God gives me new ideas, and my research shows that maybe there is a story there. Maybe I can complete this work God graciously allowed me to do. But self-confidence and adamant certainty in my own abilities are clearly lacking!

Maybe Deborah felt that way too. But if God is in a situation, if the call, the gifts, the opportunities are from Him, He will be with us. And He will guide us if we ask Him to.

We can't do life alone. We can't do the work God prepared for us to do alone. The Christian life is to be lived in community and in communion with Him, not in seclusion. If God has called us to follow Him, He will give us the grace to do whatever it is He has planned for our lives. Trust Him.

## Ponder This

When God invites us to participate in His call to share His love with the world, we are privileged and blessed if we listen. The almighty God of creation, the God who provides, the God who sees us, *wants* us. His call is His way of asking us to live life with Him both here on earth and in the eternal life that He promises to those who believe.

Such grace carries a natural (or perhaps supernatural) desire for gratitude to Him, because He could just leave us to ourselves. Believe me, we do not want God to walk away and leave us alone. There is nothing worse, no matter how many terrible things we think there could be.

Our God has not left us to ourselves. He has called us both to believe and to obey His voice. When we do, and we see the way He faithfully stays with us through every facet of life, we can be like Deborah and sing:

> Hear this, you kings! Listen, you rulers!
>> I, even I, will sing to the LORD;
>> I will praise the LORD, the God of Israel, in song.
> (Judg. 5:3 NIV)

Or as David so often sang:

> I will give thanks to the LORD because of his
>> righteousness;
>> I will sing the praises of the name of the LORD
>> Most High. (Ps. 7:17 NIV)

Praise and thanksgiving so often come in song. Did you know that God Himself sings over *us*? Music is a universal language. Music given in praise to God has the power to lift our hearts to greater joys than simple words.

> Oh sing to the LORD a new song,
>> for he has done marvelous things!
> His right hand and his holy arm
>> have worked salvation for him. (Ps. 98:1)

God loves it when we sing to Him.

## TAKING IT FURTHER

1. Have you heard that first call of God to believe in His Son, Jesus Christ? How did you respond? (If you are

in a group and want to, please share how you came to know Him.)

2. Do you realize that God has chosen you and called you to take His message of love to those He will place in your path? What kinds of opportunities has He given you to share your story with someone who is seeking to understand Jesus?

3. In a world of tolerance where truth is relative, what are some respectful ways you can still show people the love of God?

# Loving, Losing, and Waiting on God

*(Based on Ruth 1–4)*

## If I Were Ruth

The road to the burial cave blurs as I force one foot in front of the other, Naomi and Orpah clinging to me on either side. How is it possible that Mahlon and Chilion are both gone? And so soon after Naomi lost Elimelech.

My heart beats with an unsteady rhythm, and I fear I might faint along the way. But I must stay strong for Naomi's sake. Orpah's too. My sister-in-law has not been robust since the loss of her son. I am fortunate, I suppose, that in ten years of marriage I never bore Mahlon a child. If I had, the rulers of my people, who hate my foreign in-laws, might have taken him and sacrificed him on the altars of Chemosh.

I shudder at the memory of Orpah's screams when they took her son. At Naomi's bitter cries when she lost first Elimelech, then each of her sons. We are all she has left.

The cave is far from Naomi's house, and I have a strange sense of gratitude for the men of the city who were willing to carry the bodies for us. But I feel no attachment to the people here, to this place. I left this city and those in it when I chose to marry a Hebrew.

But now I am bereft of everything except these two women who hold on to me as though they can never let go. I glance at Naomi through my own tears. She is stooped and seems to have aged much in the ten years she has lived in Moab. Surely she regrets coming here, but what was a woman to do against the desires of her husband? Elimelech chose to bring his family here during the famine in Bethlehem and remained until going back seemed impossible.

Is it ever impossible to turn around and return to where you came from? What will Naomi do now?

The questions mingle with my own grief as I watch Orpah collapse in the dirt once the cave is opened. The men of the town take our husbands inside and return without them. There is no one here to say words over them except three women, and we are in no shape to do so.

The cave stone squeals as the men roll it over the opening. They wait but a moment before walking past us to return to town. Naomi sits on a nearby rock, and I sink to the earth beside her. Orpah remains some distance away, weeping.

Naomi looks at me, eyes brimming, but says nothing. I wait. What can any of us say? She has lost the most among us. I cannot imagine the intense pain coursing through her.

The sun dips lower in the sky, and I know we must start back lest wild animals find us on the way. I touch Naomi's

knee. "Mother Naomi, we should go back. It's growing dark."
I meet her hooded gaze.

"I can't go back," she says at last through a raspy voice.

Orpah's weeping stops at the words. She rises and joins me.
"We cannot stay here. We will be attacked, or worse."

Naomi nods and allows me to help her stand. We walk slowly
toward her house, each of us filled with our own dread. There
will be no men to greet after a hard day in the fields. There will
be no food prepared, as we have done no work today. I doubt
we could eat in any case.

I breathe easier when the house at last comes into view. The
sun is now quickly dropping below the horizon. I lift the latch
of the gate and usher Naomi into the dark house. Orpah lights
a lamp, and we sink to the cushions where the men used to sit.

"I meant what I said," Naomi says into the stillness that seems
to engulf us. "I cannot stay here. I am in the house with you
because I do not want to see either of you eaten by wild animals
as Elimelech was. I care nothing for myself, but I cannot bear
to lose you too."

She draws a breath, and I can see the words are hard for
her to say.

"I have heard there is food again in Bethlehem." One of the
women from the town must have heard it and told her. "When
I can get my affairs in order, perhaps sell the land back to the
man Elimelech purchased it from, I will return to my home.
My real home. I can no longer abide this land. It has taken
everything I love . . ." She paused. "Except you." She looked
from me to Orpah.

We glance at each other. "We will go with you," I am quick
to assure her. "We cannot let you go alone."

"No, we cannot," Orpah agrees. But I hear the hesitance in
her voice.

Both of us have lived in Moab all of our lives. It was here that we found our first loves, even though they were not men of Moab. How can we possibly leave all that we know? And yet with one glance at the woman who has been more mother to me than my own, I feel a sense of deep resolve fill me. How can I possibly stay? She is all I have.

## What We Know

Have you ever lost someone really close to you? We have a number of widows in my family, and I have friends who have lost their husbands. I dread the day that could happen to me.

Ruth watched her father-in-law die, and then she lost her husband and her brother-in-law, probably fairly close together. The Bible tells us that after Naomi and her family had lived in Moab about ten years, both of her sons had died. We don't know how long Ruth had been married to Mahlon before his death. But short or long, grief is grief, and it had to be hard on her. It was Ruth's choice to go to Bethlehem with her mother-in-law, which makes her stand out to us.

If you put yourself in Ruth's place, could you have followed your mother-in-law back to her hometown, away from everything you knew? What would you do if the people there didn't accept you? What would happen when the only person you knew died?

(Side note: In Ruth's day, it was common practice for the new wife to live with her husband's family. For Ruth to choose Naomi over her own mother, if she still lived, would not have seemed unusual in that sense. This tradition is foreign to Western thinking, although some cultures still practice this. I have Middle Eastern and certain European neighbors who do this very thing. One son brought his wife to live with him and his parents. Two other houses on our block are homes to three generations all living under one roof.)

Ruth was a strong woman, but even strong women can have doubts. If she did, her convictions won out over them. She took a risk to leave Moab and all she knew behind her. Perhaps it was because she had no one else left to love there. Or maybe she had come to know the God of the Hebrews and no longer wanted anything to do with the child-sacrificing god of her people. Whatever the reason, her words to Naomi that decision-making day have been read at weddings ever since (though in a different context). I have a plaque with the words engraved in stone on my mantel above the fireplace:

Do not urge me to leave you or to return from following you. For where you go I will go, and where you lodge I will lodge. Your people shall be my people, and your God my God. Where you die I will die, and there will I be buried. May the LORD do so to me and more also if anything but death parts me from you. (Ruth 1:16–17)

Pretty strong commitment. We commend Ruth for her loyalty. Despite her losses, she knew what it meant to love. I think we can learn a lot from her.

She promised to go with Naomi. She promised to stay with her. She promised to follow Naomi's God. And she promised to be buried with her. Only death could part them.

Some of our marriages need such commitment, don't they?

I do not know of a modern-day example of Ruth. Too many of our families are fractured, and mothers and daughters or mothers-in-law and daughters-in-law are of such different generations that we often don't relate well. Values change from generation to generation, and it takes love and understanding to look past our differences and find things we do have in common if we want good relationships.

Ruth chose to follow Naomi's culture, her values, and her God. Today, except for those few cultures named above, we see a lot more of the opposite of that, don't we? I think both generations need to find ways to communicate our differences and tear down walls that might divide us. Forgive as we have been forgiven. Love unconditionally. And don't try to tell the other person what to do. That's hard for us as parents when our adult kids no longer need parenting, but it's not our job to train them anymore. God gives us a window of time to teach and emulate His love and guide our children to know Him and love Him, and we do our best. But our children are not going to be clones of us. (Boy, am I glad that's true!) They are going to have their own opinions, and like Ruth, they will have to decide for themselves whether they will follow what they were taught.

Naomi likely taught Ruth about the Hebrew God, because there was no one else who could have taught her except her husband. She wouldn't have come to know Him from her family or her Moabite culture. But we don't know if Ruth believed in Him until she made that declaration of allegiance to Naomi.

No matter how young or old your children are, they are going to have to make that declaration of whether or not to follow Jesus on their own. God is a personal God, and as many have said, "He has no grandchildren." He adopts anyone who will come to Him and believe—then they become His child, like Ruth did—but it has to be their own decision.

If your children are more like Orpah than Ruth and go back to a life of idol worship, there is only one thing you can do. Pray. Entrust them to God as you did when they were babies and let Him be the one to pursue them. He is a loving

Father and the Good Shepherd, and He loves your children more than you do.

We have absolutely no control over these situations. We never did. We think we control our lives, but as Ruth and Naomi discovered, there is no control except over our own decisions. And even those are sometimes out of our power, because circumstances can destroy the things we wanted to do.

Once Ruth made that decision to follow Naomi and her people and her God, she found herself in some pretty strange situations. She ended up gleaning in a field and lying down beside a man's feet in order to propose marriage—all because her mother-in-law asked her to. I'm pretty sure that scenario hasn't happened quite that way since!

But once the man, Boaz, agreed to pursue the possibility of marriage to this dedicated foreign woman, Ruth found herself in another place that I think we can all relate to—waiting on God.

## Imagine with Me

The grain Boaz placed in my scarf weighs me down as I hurry through Bethlehem's darkened streets. I tighten my grip, fearful of dropping any of the precious food. Naomi will be so pleased! But my heart pounds with anticipation and fear.

I know I should not be afraid, but it is hard not to worry that something will go wrong. Perhaps Boaz will think about what I have done and change his mind—such a brazen act to lay at a man's feet as he sleeps. And I an unmarried woman! But Naomi has assured me this was the right thing to do. Perhaps her people are used to such strange customs.

The house looms close now, and I rush toward it, careful of the burden I carry. I sweep into the courtyard and open the door to our house. A light burns within, and Naomi, who seems as though she has not slept, greets me.

"Let me help you with that." She moves as quickly as her aging bones will allow and drags a large earthenware pot closer to me.

I carefully lower the end of my scarf, and the grain spills into the pot, filling it to the top. Naomi claps her hands like a young girl.

"So much! The man will surely act if he gave you such a generous gift." She beams at me.

I look at the pot, now wishing Naomi had not moved it, but I do not complain. She wants to help, and she can do so little. I bend down to drag the pot back across the floor, grateful once again to the God of the Hebrews for looking on us with such kindness.

"Now tell me everything." Naomi is at my side again, and once the pot is in place, she takes my hand and pulls me toward the sitting room.

I draw a breath, grateful to rest my legs. "I did as you said. I waited until the man was asleep, then I crept to where he lay and uncovered his feet and lay beside him until he awoke. I know I startled him, but he did not cry out. He spoke in whispers, and when I told him who I was and why I was there, he thanked me for not going after the younger men. He considers it a kindness that I would ask him instead of someone else." I pause, still uncertain and fearful. "But what do I do now, Mother Naomi? I am anxious, and I want to know. Does he truly want me? When will he tell us?"

Naomi holds up a hand to stop my rushing words. "Wait, my daughter, until you learn how the matter turns out, for the man will not rest but will settle the matter today."

I nod, though my heart still races. I stand, unable to sit still. Why is waiting so hard?

Together we climb to the roof of the house and look toward the city gate, where Boaz must conduct this business of marriage to Mahlon's widow. I know everything must be done correctly. What if the man who is a closer relative than Boaz wants to marry me instead? *Oh God of Abraham, please do not let it be so.*

I have come to care for Boaz these many months working in his fields. I cannot imagine another man holding me as Mahlon once did. I pace the roof as Naomi waits at the parapet, shaking her head at me. I know she is more patient than I. Perhaps that is something one learns with age.

But as the sun creeps over the horizon and moves across the sky, I feel no more patient than I did when I rushed through Bethlehem's dark streets. Waiting on men is not easy. And even when I pray, I do not find that waiting grows easier.

## From Waiting to Trust

Have you ever obsessed about something? I have. Through the years, I've obsessed about so many different things—from what to wear for a special occasion to how to react to a difficult situation to frustration over another person's actions.

We all fret over things in life. It's easy to make our worries the central focus of our thoughts. But when we do that, especially when we have to wait for something or someone, we lose our peace.

The thing is, obsessing about stuff is worry. Or anxiety, if you prefer that word, and the rate of anxiety even among children today is a lot higher than it was when I was growing up. Anxiety can lead to many troubling issues, from irritability to sleeplessness to high blood pressure to inability to cope with life and so much more. I'm not an expert on the subject by any means, but I sure know what it feels like to be anxious. It's not a fun place to be.

I discovered one day as I was praying that anxiety is really fear in disguise. So I asked myself, *What is it that I fear?* And then I told God about those fears.

I think people don't really talk to God in an intimate, honest way, even as believers in Christ, because we don't really trust Him. I mean, we might have prayed a prayer asking Him to keep us from going to hell, especially if we were raised in church and taught what the Bible says about heaven, hell, faith, and what Jesus did for us on the cross so we could be set free from sin. But just because we trust Him with our far-off eternity doesn't mean we trust Him with our day-to-day anxieties. I know I am guilty of not letting go of that anxiety factor.

Once I realized that anxiety is fear, however, I have been able to identify my fears the moment I sense anxiety knocking on my heart's door. That doesn't mean I'm always great at giving those fears to God. Sometimes I just want things to change, or I want to see God act in a way that I think He should right now, not when He's ready. That can also cause me to obsess over those things where He is telling me, "Wait, my daughter."

That happened to me not too long ago during one of those days when I was trying to work but couldn't get my mind off something that was troubling me. I was working and praying, but my work was suffering from obsession praying. *I* was suffering from obsession overload.

But as I listened to the Holy Spirit speak to my heart, I heard Him say, "Fix your eyes on Jesus, the Author and Finisher of your faith." Then I recalled a verse in the Old Testament that says, "You will keep in perfect peace those whose minds are steadfast, because they trust in you" (Isa. 26:3 NIV).

70

In that moment, I decided to stop focusing on what was troubling me and focus instead on Jesus. Every time that other obsession tried to replace Jesus, I looked again to Him. And you know what? Perfect peace really does come when Jesus is our focus.

If Ruth did worry that day about what would happen with Boaz, she would not have known much peace. Of course, we can't know for sure how she felt, only that Naomi told her, "Wait, my daughter."

*Wait, my daughter.* Waiting is so hard. We know that. We live it every day. And trust me, waiting doesn't grow easier with age.

But I don't think patience comes with aging. Patience and the ability to wait on God come through trials and persevering through them. They grow through difficult times in our lives when we *could* let anxiety rule our hearts, but instead we focus our minds on Jesus and let His peace rule.

It sounds so simple, but we're human. And nobody likes the word "patience." It's joked about in Christian circles as a bad thing, but I think God finds it very attractive. I think it pleases Him immensely when we trust Him enough to wait on His timing, to wait for Him to get us out of our struggles when He knows we are ready—when we've passed the test, learned the lesson, and grown to be more like Jesus (James 1:2–5).

For some reason, God uses the trials of life as the means of maturing us. There is something about humbling ourselves and waiting on God that teaches us that life isn't all about us. We are not the center of the universe, and we don't have to always have things our way.

Tell that to a child and she'll throw a tantrum. Tell that to an adult and hopefully he won't throw a tantrum. Tell that to a maturing Christian and maybe, just maybe, she'll nod and smile and accept God's plan, because she knows it's perfect and much better than her own.

Ruth came out of Moab with all of the baggage of a false religion whose standards she couldn't meet. That's what religions do. They set standards no one can meet. But she came to know the God of Abraham, Isaac, and Jacob and found that she didn't have to change who she was to be accepted by Him. She simply had to trust Him and follow where He led her.

Trust and obey. There's an old hymn by that title. In part the song says,

> When we walk with the Lord in the light of His
>   Word,
> What a glory He sheds on our way!
> While we do His good will, He abides with us still,
> And with all who will trust and obey.
>
> Trust and obey, for there's no other way
> To be happy in Jesus, but to trust and obey.
>
> Then in fellowship sweet we will sit at His feet.
> Or we'll walk by His side in the way.
> What He says we will do, where He sends we will go;
> Never fear, only trust and obey.
>
> John H. Sammis, "Trust and Obey"

## Ponder This

Losing people we love is one of the most painful things we can suffer on this earth. But if we don't risk our hearts to love others, we actually lose more than we would if we took a chance on love.

Waiting on God is one of the most difficult things we can ever do in this life. But we are going to be asked to do so over and over again until we meet Jesus face-to-face, because God uses that waiting to make us like Him. We can't get to that point any other way. It's a journey of faith, and we don't reach maturity overnight. We get it by waiting on God, one day at a time.

Psalm 27:14 says this:

> Wait for the LORD;
>> be strong, and let your heart take courage;
>> wait for the LORD!

Loving someone takes courage because we risk our hearts. Losing something or someone takes courage to live through because loss is always devastating. Waiting on God takes courage because we don't know how long the wait will be.

Each one of these courageous acts involves our hearts. A heart devoted to the Lord is one that will take up these challenges. That doesn't mean we will never falter or find ourselves crying out to God for help. It simply means that when we need Him, and even if we think we don't, God is with us. He will see us through.

## TAKING IT FURTHER

1. Have you ever been in a place where you were not willing to risk love for fear of possible loss? On the flip side, have you ever risked loving someone and had your heart broken? In either case, would you say it is better to have loved and lost or to never have loved at all? Why?

2. What do you think of Ruth's decision to follow her mother-in-law to a strange land and to embrace a God

she had not known before? Could you have done what Ruth did? Why or why not?

3. Are you in a place of waiting on God for something in your life? How does that make you feel? Can you share a time when you waited or didn't wait on God's timing and what the outcome was—good or bad?

# Naomi

## When Turning Around
## Is the Best Thing

*(Based on Ruth 1–4)*

### If I Were Naomi

I have lived a hard life. I did not expect my life to go the way
it has, and I would have chosen a different path if it had been
up to me. But women do not talk their husbands out of what
they have determined they are going to do. Some might. But
I knew my Elimelech would never listen to my admonitions
to wait and see if God would lift the famine.

I wish we had never moved to Moab. I stand now at the
edge of the courtyard of the home we built here, staring at
the sun as it makes its descent to the west. The house has held
up since Elimelech's passing, but with Mahlon and Chilion
gone, there is no way I can keep things together, plant the

fields, and care for our daily needs, even with the help of my daughters-in-law.

They should return to their families in any case. But I cannot yet bear to part with them. The burial of my sons is still too fresh, and a knot forms in my middle as I fight the urge to weep yet again.

How bitterly the Almighty has dealt with me! And the questions continue to plague me. Why? What have I done to deserve this fate, to be the one who remains alive when nearly everyone I love is dead?

Muffled voices come from inside the house, and I turn to look through the open door. Orpah and Ruth sit on the cushions, talking quietly. They are grieving my sons as well, but they do not grieve as I do. They do not know that the hand of God is against me. If it were not for me, they would have married men of Moab. Surely I have been sinful from birth. Surely I somehow angered my God. Why else would He take away all that I hold dear?

Never mind that my husband brought us here. Never mind that I wanted to talk him out of it. I eventually resigned myself to coming and staying even after his death. How was I supposed to fight against both sons when they were determined to marry those women?

A sigh bursts forth, a weight trying to escape my chest. But the sigh does nothing to remove the heavy load of guilt and shame I bear.

"Mother Naomi?" Ruth's voice calls to me, and I walk as an aged woman, for that is what I am now, to the sitting room.

"Yes, my daughter?" I close the door and slowly lower myself onto one of the cushions. Light flickers from the clay lamps, giving us little glow now that the sun has set.

"Will you eat something?" Ruth passes a tray of flatbread and cheese to me, left over from earlier today.

I shake my head. "I am not hungry." Will I ever desire food again? Fresh sorrow wells within me. I let the tears fall briefly, then look from one girl to the other. "As you know, we have done what we could to sell this land, but the man Elimelech paid for the right to live here claims he owes me nothing. He will reclaim the land, and the money my husband gave him is lost to me." I pause, searching each dear face. "So tomorrow I will return to my homeland. Perhaps there I can find someone who yet remembers me." My people know how to take care of widows, if only I can get there without harm coming to me.

Silence follows my remark. Ruth is the first to respond. "It will work out, Mother Naomi. We will join you and work in Bethlehem to support ourselves, as we would have done here." She lifts her chin, her gaze certain.

"Yes. We will find work in Bethlehem." Orpah's response is not as convincing.

"Before we leave, might I go into the city for provisions and to say goodbye to my family?" Ruth asks me.

"Yes, I would like to do the same." Orpah's eyes carry the shadow of wistfulness.

I do not hesitate, for I cannot imagine making the trip without them. "I think we can wait a day or two for you both to do as you have asked. Perhaps if your families have any provisions to spare . . ." I cannot finish as it hits me like a millstone to the gut just how poor I have suddenly become.

"I will see if I can help with that," Ruth promises.

"Very well. Thank you." I force myself up and move toward my chambers. "I am very tired. Tomorrow you may visit your families."

As I lay on my pallet that night, however, I wonder how wise are my words. To go home again will be to go in humiliation, for we left with plenty and I will be returning empty. Is there anyone who will truly remember me, take me in?

I don't know whether I still have living relatives or not. But I have a deep compulsion to return to my roots. I do not belong in this foreign land. The God of my people dwells in Israel's lands, not in Moab's. I have listened to foolish choices long enough.

## What We Know

Naomi's story is well told in the book of Ruth. In fact, we learn more of Naomi in that book than we do of Ruth.

Naomi, whose name means "pleasant," moved with her husband, Elimelech, and her two sons, Mahlon and Chilion, to the land of Moab during a famine in Bethlehem. She lost all of her men while living in that land. I feel she was a female Job, for her losses were surely as great emotionally, though on a much smaller physical scale.

She left full and returned empty. If anyone had reason to say her glass was half empty, Naomi did. Indeed, she grew bitter and asked those who remembered her to call her Mara, meaning "bitter." Her soul ached with the bitter taste of grief.

I think in some respect we can all relate to Naomi. If not now, someday we will. When faced with her grief, Naomi couldn't push forward and keep living in Moab. Moab represented all she had lost. So she went back home.

Looking back is not a popular practice today. In fact, we are told often to keep moving forward, to press on, to reach for the golden ring or the pot of gold at the end of the rainbow. To run the race, to never look back. Going back holds a lot of negative connotations, not only in our day but also in Scripture.

The apostle Paul said,

> But one thing I do: forgetting what lies behind and straining forward to what lies ahead, I press on toward the goal for the prize of the upward call of God in Christ Jesus. Let those of us who are mature think this way, and if in anything you think otherwise, God will reveal that also to you. (Phil. 3:13–15)

Paul was looking ahead toward the goal of knowing Christ, of completing the work he had been given, of finishing the race marked out for him. This should be the goal of every believer who wants to truly follow Christ. Our lives are not in what is past. We are here to please the Lord and look forward to the joy of being with Christ, which is far greater than anything we may suffer here on earth.

Yet in Isaiah 46:8–10, God says,

> Remember this and stand firm,
>> recall it to mind, you transgressors,
>> remember the former things of old;
> for I am God, and there is no other;
>> I am God, and there is none like me,
> declaring the end from the beginning
>> and from ancient times things not yet done,
> saying, "My counsel shall stand,
>> and I will accomplish all my purpose."

Sometimes God tells us to forget what is past, and sometimes He wants us to remember it. So how do we tell the difference? When is it better to look back or to *go* back than it is to keep moving forward?

As I write this, spring is trying desperately to push its way forward and allow us to forget the long Michigan winter. We in the Midwest are quite ready for flowers and sunshine and birds and beauty to burst forth once again. This is a time of year when I want to look forward, not back.

In a sense, I think life is like the seasons. When we are small, we can't wait to grow up. We are constantly moving forward. I remember being thirteen going on sixteen and sixteen going on twenty-one. We want to skip ahead when we are young, then we reach a certain age and think, *Wait! Slow down!*

The truth is, when we are young, we feel invincible and often have a great passion for life—to live it *now!* None of us want to look back at the past. That's for old people! Yet God in His wisdom designed festivals for the people of Israel so that they would be forced to remember events of the past.

Passover recalls the Exodus from Egypt. For Christians, communion recalls Jesus' death, burial, and resurrection. Sometimes God told the Israelites to set up stones to mark a place where something significant happened. When He parted the Jordan for them to cross on dry land, He told them to take stones from the river and set them up for each of the twelve tribes. And when their children asked about those stones, the Israelites would tell them about what God had done for them at the Jordan as they were entering the Promised Land.

In a similar way, God wants us to remember what He has done for us so that we will teach our children of His goodness to us. Looking back for that reason is a very good thing.

In Naomi's case, however, she wasn't looking back to remember. She wanted to return to a place she knew, something familiar. I don't think Naomi's attitude was like Lot's wife, who couldn't let go of what she was told to release. Naomi was going back to regain what she'd lost. Perhaps she felt as though the foreign land in which she resided proved her family's disobedience to Yahweh.

If you have read the book of Ruth, you know that when Naomi returned to Bethlehem she was destitute. She needed help. Home was the only place that might offer that help.

To lose everything and everyone you love is unimaginably devastating.

Horatio G. Spafford (1828–1888) was a devoted Christian and a successful lawyer and businessman from Chicago. His wife, Anna, had given him five children. One young son died of pneumonia in 1871. Shortly after, the great Chicago fire of 1871 took all of Spafford's fortune in a single night. He was able to rebuild his business, but he could not have seen what lay around the next bend.

Two years after the fire, he sent his wife and four daughters to Europe on a French ocean liner. He had planned to go with them, but a business problem kept him in Chicago. He would join them later.

On November 21, 1873, the ocean liner collided with another ship. Of the 313 passengers on board, 226 perished, including all four of the Spaffords' daughters. His wife was the only one who survived.

Such tragedy seems beyond comprehension. Though we hear of tragedy on the news every night, few of us face it on such a grand scale.

Naomi faced such tragedy. While most people would equate Spafford's tragedy to Job's, Naomi was not much different. In each case, God eventually brought great comfort, but I doubt any of these people truly understood what their suffering would produce in them and in others until they met Christ in eternity.

Life is like that for all of us. We all go through times of loss, some greater than others. And there are different types of losses. Sometimes we suffer more than one at a time.

The day I first worked on this chapter, dear friends of ours lost a husband, father, brother. About a month ago, one of our pastors lost a son. We've lost neighbors and jobs and seen relationships fall apart. We've watched friends go through things too painful to even discuss—from rape to devastating illness to estrangement.

I think Naomi did hang on to one thing in the midst of her tragedies. She kept at least a thread of hope and a desperate faith that God had not completely abandoned her. For surely she could have felt abandoned. Isn't it easy to feel that way when the hard things in life come?

Yet Naomi's life is different than Job's. She wasn't the subject of a divine test. Her husband made decisions that led them away from their homeland, like the prodigal son left his father's house to live in a distant land. Neither her husband nor the prodigal trusted God with their futures.

Could Naomi have returned to Bethlehem with her sons after her husband's death? What prevented her from doing so? God doesn't tell us that detail. But like the prodigal son who lost everything his father had given him and found himself in a place he didn't want to be, then decided to go back to his father, she came to her senses and returned home.

Jacob's son Judah made a similar decision to leave home after he had convinced his brothers to sell their younger brother Joseph to Ishmaelite traders. Judah returned to his father with a lie about what had happened to Joseph, Jacob's favorite son, but he didn't plan on his father's reaction to the loss. I suspect that Judah couldn't live with the guilt, so he went to live among the Canaanites, married, had kids, and lost his wife and two of his three sons. It took him about twenty years—Naomi not quite as long—to come to his senses and return to his father. He returned a changed man, a humbler man. Naomi returned a changed woman—a bitter woman.

There are times in our lives when the right thing *is* to go back. Maybe we have left a relationship broken, and we know it is on us to fix it. We might not have been the only one to break that relationship, but if we don't return, there will be no healing.

Have you been there? I have.

There have been times when I knew I had hurt someone or I felt responsible to heal a rift I didn't understand. I needed to take that first step because I had said the words, intentionally or not, and I had to make it right.

Have you ever been in that place where God was whispering to your heart, "Be reconciled to your brother" (Matt. 5:24) or some other verse that convicted you because you knew He was right? That's not a fun place to be, is it?

It takes courage and a lot of grace to be the one to make that phone call. I know people who cannot or simply will not do so. Sometimes even the death or impending death of a loved one is not a strong enough reason to give us that courage. I think that's because courage to truly apologize or accept someone else's apology is a grace that God gives us when we ask Him. We can't fix things on our own.

That's not to say every broken thing can be mended, because it can't. Naomi couldn't get her husband or sons back from the dead just by returning home. What she could get was a chance to rejoin her people and be reunited with her God. To live among them meant to worship God in the way He intended His people to worship Him. And she wasn't living in a place where that was possible.

What she was really going back for, in my opinion, was to make things right in her life with God. In the process of going back to where she knew she belonged, she gained an entirely new family and a lot of love from the people she had left behind.

Sometimes life surprises us that way. When we have the courage as Naomi did to take that first step, to turn around, to change our minds, to make that call, to humble our attitudes, we just might find joy waiting for us on the other side.

## Imagine with Me

I sit in the shade of the courtyard where the sun slants across the cut stones but does not reach us where we are nestled. In my arms I cradle a new babe that my Ruth has given to me. The wonder of Obed's birth still causes me to look toward the heavens and feel my heart lighten with gratitude. *Thank You.* It is a prayer to my God, for He has indeed been far more gracious to me than I could have ever imagined.

When I was living life, raising a family first in Bethlehem and then in Moab, I could not have seen this day coming even if I had tried. I could not have imagined the joys and sorrows that awaited me until they had come and gone.

I never thought I would hear a child's voice call to me, "Savta." I never expected to hold a babe again and feel such love, such aching joy, knowing he is mine. He is Ruth and Boaz's son, of course, but by the laws of our people, he is the son of my Mahlon.

The women of the town say, "Naomi has a son." I know he is not mine to raise or nurse, but I will teach him. I will tell him of our God and of the things we were taught to remember—of all the good things our God has done for Israel. I will remind Obed that though we live in difficult times—for without a strong leader as in the days of Moses and Joshua, we are often under assault by foreign kings—our God is still true.

Didn't He take care of Ruth and of me? Two poor, destitute women, and one a foreigner?

I'm glad I listened to the longing in my heart to return home, to return to my people, to my God. I had always known that He was the only God and that my husband had put us in harm's way when he settled us among a people of foreign gods. For a time I nearly lost my faith. I had surely lost my hope.

But my God has been faithful to me, and I sit here now, rocking Obed as he sleeps in my arms, looking in awe at his innocent beauty. He knows nothing of life or hurt or sorrow or joy. He will learn soon enough, but for now he knows only the bliss of infant sleep.

And I know the joy of innocence regained. For my folly and my loss have been removed, my shame of our choices gone, ever since God looked once again with kindness on Ruth and on me. He gave her Boaz, and He gave all of us Obed.

Coming home was not easy. I nearly faltered and turned away from the road to Bethlehem more than once, but Ruth held me steady. It hurt to see the women greet me as if I should be a happy woman, for I was still too bitter to see that coming back was the best choice I could have made. But now . . . now I know that they saw what I could not. God led me to make this journey, and it has been worth every step back. Sometimes it is good to come home. I am very glad that I did.

## From Past Failure to Future Joy

It is not hard for me to imagine what Naomi might have felt when she left Bethlehem with her family. We are not told whether she wanted to leave, but I can bet that she wanted to remain with her family. If her husband wanted to find respite from the famine in Moab and her boys were going with him, she wasn't about to be left behind. That's how I would have felt. (Of course, my husband wouldn't have just picked up and said, "We're moving" without our discussing it first and agreeing on it together.)

It's so easy to focus on our past failures, isn't it? We all experience failure in our lives. It's part of life. We do things even as believers in Christ that we know displease God. Sometimes we know the truth, but the lie is so tempting that we make excuses as to why it's not so bad. We give in because we want to. Maybe we even pray about it, but some things do not need our prayers when we already know the answer. Since God said, "Do not murder," then He's not going to change His mind on that if we ask Him if it's okay.

I know that's a bit extreme, but let's look at an example that is closer to home for most of the world: sex before marriage, or sex outside of marriage in any form. God's Word says, "Don't do it." But we are tempted. It can be very easy to give in to that temptation because it wars against our hearts.

Gina (a fictional name that combines more than one story) knew that feeling. Her husband hadn't been attentive in a long time, and when he thought she wasn't looking, he was on the internet viewing pictures that turned her stomach. Was she not enough for him? Why would he need *that* when he had her? She began to feel distant from him, and she forgot to guard her own heart. It was hard to guard a hurting heart. It was so much easier to listen to the guy who flirted with her and told her how pretty she was. Red flags should have gone up, but she was already justifying her feelings.

Joseph and Judah knew those feelings too. Both men were tempted by women who were not their wives. One fled the temptation. (He did not stop to pray about it. He ran.) The other initiated the liaison and got the woman pregnant out of wedlock.

All of the justification in the world doesn't help us when we give in to what we know is wrong. Then we find ourselves falling into failure, like Naomi's sons marrying foreign women. In Nehemiah 13:26–27 we read,

> Did not Solomon king of Israel sin on account of such women? Among the many nations there was no king like him, and he was beloved by his God, and God made him king over all Israel. Nevertheless, foreign women made even him to sin. Shall we then listen to you and do all this great evil and act treacherously against our God by marrying foreign women?

While God did make exceptions for foreign believing women such as Rahab and Ruth, His general rule was for His people to marry within their clans, to preserve their tribal lands and to keep from being tempted by foreign gods that their wives might have worshiped. (Remember, behind every foreign god a demon lurks, as we discussed in chapter 2.)

Naomi's sons married foreign women rather than return to Israel to find wives. The impression this gives us is that they were happy to settle in this foreign land with its foreign ways and foreign gods. There is no mention of them asking the God of Israel what to do.

Until Ruth came to believe in the Hebrew God, Naomi probably blamed herself for her sons' choices. A lot of mothers do that, whether the blame is theirs or not. But those young men were responsible for their own decisions.

Naomi could have looked at her life in Moab as a complete failure. If I had traveled to a distant land and lost my husband

and sons, I would feel like life was over, as though there was nothing left to hope in or hope for.

And yet, something led Naomi to return home. To look back and think that maybe there was something left in her life that would turn out for good. So she changed her thinking and turned around and took the long walk back to Bethlehem with Ruth at her side.

I doubt very much that Naomi even imagined the future joy that awaited her. She could not have known what would happen to Ruth, or that Boaz would be free to marry Ruth or even want to do so. She was going home in sorrow and bitterness, but God turned that sorrow into joy.

Have you been there? Has there been a time when you took a step of faith, not knowing where it would lead, and discovered that God was with you all along? He saw your sorrow, your bitterness, your pain, and though you might have blamed Him for the cause of them, He wasn't the one who hurt you. He is the one who gave everything to show you that He loves you.

I remember a time when I longed for something and it seemed as though it would never happen. Sometimes we can pray and nothing seems to change. Years and years go by, and we still wait. Waiting like that can cause us to despair or give up. We decide that God isn't listening, so what good does it do to pray? Or we just grow weary and can't take another step forward in faith. We lose hope.

And then one day, we see a complete turnaround.

That happened to me after twenty years of waiting to sell my first book. I had written a prayer in my journal—a prayer of despair that told the Lord I was on the brink of quitting. Twenty years of rejection is hard to take. Sometimes we just don't have the grit to keep moving forward. So I figured perhaps I had misread God's plan for me. Maybe I wasn't meant to be a writer after all. So I gave my desire to Him and nearly forgot about that prayer. I only thought about it once or twice after that. I just went on with life. What else could I do? I couldn't *make* a publisher want me. I'd certainly tried long enough, as had my agent.

And then one day I got that phone call. We had a publishing contract!

A similar situation, though not as long a wait, happened years earlier when I wanted a baby and suffered a miscarriage after a year of disappointment. (Sometimes we just don't understand why, do we?) But when I discovered I was pregnant on vacation in Hawaii, there wasn't anything quite like that feeling! It wasn't supposed to happen, but God surprised me. There were a lot of little miracles with that child.

Maybe you're in a situation of trying desperately to find the right job—any job! Or your child is sicker than you could have possibly imagined. Or you just came from seeing a divorce lawyer because your spouse wouldn't go to a marriage counselor with you. Or your child did something that has you reeling, or she's struggling with problems that are too big and you can't help her.

Recently I watched my neighbor burn tree limbs in his backyard, something that is not legal in our city. Maybe because he had the fire enclosed, it was fine. Maybe he had called to check ahead of time. (He hadn't and it wasn't okay, we later learned.) The scary thing was that, had there been any wind, those embers could have spread. We were all fortunate that nothing bad came from his poor decision other than a fine.

In that Chicago fire of 1871, the winds were not quiet, and they took that fire and destroyed a huge part of the city. Horatio Spafford lost everything overnight. And he continued to lose people he loved. Though he still experienced good, life brought a lot of pain.

But out of his pain, he penned one of the most comforting and famous songs still sung today, "It Is Well with My Soul." Perhaps you've heard of it, but let me quote the words, because one thing I believe God wants us to remember is this: He can bring amazing joy and good beyond understanding even among the ashes of our lives. When everything seems bleak, when something seems beyond impossible to fix, our God can do anything. He's really good at fixing things, at taking what is broken and making it brand new. He takes the people society has forgotten or given up on and breathes new life into them. It *can* be well with our souls when they are right with Him.

> When peace, like a river, attendeth my way,
> When sorrows like sea billows roll;
> Whatever my lot, Thou hast taught me to say,
> It is well, it is well with my soul.
>
> It is well with my soul,
> It is well, it is well with my soul.
>
> And Lord, haste the day when the faith shall be sight,
> The clouds be rolled back as a scroll;
> The trump shall resound, and the Lord shall descend,
> Even so, it is well with my soul.

## Ponder This

God is in the business of bringing joy. He wants us to know His love, and when I think about how great that love is, it staggers me. I was thinking about it the other day in relation to how much love I have for my own children. And then I thought, *If I love my children this much, how does God feel toward me?*

When we stray from the place God wants us to be and we know that moving forward can't happen until we go back and make things right with Him, remember that He is wooing us to return to Him. God's love for us is eternal. His longing for us to walk with Him in truth is unending. Third John 4 tells us:

> I have no greater joy than to hear that my children are walking in the truth.

If we can feel that way about our physical or spiritual children, it is only because it's a reflection of how God sees us. He wants us, His adopted spiritual children, to walk in truth with Him.

Sometimes that means we need to return to our roots and find again what we have lost. Naomi went home when she thought she had nothing left, and she found that she still had much joy ahead of her. But she could only find that joy by going back, by going home to what she knew was true. The same lesson applies to each of us.

## TAKING IT FURTHER

1. Have you ever walked away from what you knew was true? What happened as a result? Did you ever find a reason to return?

2. How has life disappointed you? Can you point to decisions you have made that led to consequences you didn't imagine? What can you do, by God's grace, to

let God turn those disappointments into something good?

3. Have you ever lost someone close to you? How has God comforted you during your season of grief? Can you sing "It Is Well with My Soul" and mean it?

# Hannah

## Never Giving Up on God

*(Based on 1 Samuel 1–2)*

### If I Were Hannah

The cries of a newborn pierce the waning light of sunset. My rival—my husband's *other* wife, Peninnah—has given birth again. And my heart aches with the sound as it has every other time.

I should be used to the shouts of celebration, the cheers of the men, the loud praise of Peninnah's mother and Elkanah's mother as they exclaim over another boy, but I fear I will never grow used to them. Perhaps if Peninnah were a kind woman, one who wanted my help or shared her children with me, things would be different.

But as I turn from the window where I can see the shadows of the family gathered around her courtyard, I know she will never change. Peninnah wants Elkanah's love, which is the one thing I hold, so she taunts me, trying to get me to complain to him. At least I assume that is her reason for hating me as she does.

A sigh I've held too long escapes, and I walk to the back of my house, where a door leads to the river and the woods beyond. I come here often to pray, but sometimes, on days like today, I wonder if God hears the desperate cries of a lonely woman's heart.

I have believed in Him since I sat on my father's knee and listened to him tell the stories of our forefathers. I know our God is great. He has done great and mighty deeds for Israel, from the time He called our father Abraham until Moses led our people out of Egypt and Joshua conquered the Promised Land. But that does not mean He is concerned about the longings of someone like me.

Even in the times in which we live, when judges some-times rule, we have seen His deliverance and miraculous hand. But those times have been few, and most of them involved great wars when God delivered our people from a cruel enemy.

Elkanah and I believe we need such a deliverer again, not because of a foreign enemy but because of the corrupt priests who lead our people. Sometimes I wonder if I am blessed not to have children because of the times in which we live.

I kick at a fallen branch that blocks my path and listen to the soothing rush of water that moves beside me. I hear in my memory the cry of Peninnah's newborn. I cannot deny my heart's cry. Corrupt times or not, I long to give Elkanah a child. But God does not listen to my desperate prayers, not even when they come with a sacrifice.

*Why, Lord? Will You forget me forever?*

I know it is still possible. I am young yet, and our fore-mothers—most of whom were barren for many years—eventually birthed a child. God could still hear my prayers. I believe He can do the impossible. But I don't know if He will.

That is the part that fills me with anguish and tortures my thoughts when Peninnah bears another child. I do not understand why I am overlooked. Why I am forgotten. Like Rachel of old. I understand her pain as she watched her sister have child after child. I could give my maid to Elkanah as she did, but I will not do it. My maid deserves a home of her own, when she is old enough for me to seek a man for her in marriage.

No. I cannot be so selfish.

As I sink to the dirt and let my feet dangle near the river's swiftly moving waters, I wonder if praying really makes any difference. I have done everything I can to obey the law, and I believe despite the hurt. But I admit my faith wavers at times, and my hope grows thinner with each passing year.

I glance at the last vestiges of orange and gold, the sun on its way to its place in the west. *Do You see me? Do my prayers matter to You at all? Or should I stop asking and learn to be content with my life as it is?*

I want to know. I truly want to do what He would have for me. But there is no response to my silent pleas.

As I trudge back to my home and light a lamp against the night, I try to shut out the sounds of celebration. Elkanah will come to me soon, and I must be cheerful for him. He won't expect it of me. But I have determined to be pleasing to him even when my heart is breaking. For if I do to Peninnah as she has done to me, he might love her more. And then I will have lost everything.

## What We Know

Hannah lived during the time when the judges ruled Israel. First Samuel 1 tells us that she was married to Elkanah, who also had another wife, Peninnah. First Chronicles 6 tells us that Elkanah was of the tribe of Levi. We also know that he lived in the hill country of Ephraim.

Peninnah had many children, but Hannah was barren—a familiar theme in the Bible. Many women who played prominent roles later in their lives began their marriages in barrenness. But every time, God had a purpose for making them wait. When at last they bore a child, that child either came in an impossible way (think Sarah) or became a mighty man of God (think John the Baptist). While waiting was surely painful for those women, the children they bore brought great blessing not only to Israel but to the world.

Hannah lived at a time when the leadership, the priesthood in particular, was ultra-corrupt. We can only imagine how that affected Hannah and her family. I explored her dilemma and possible scenarios in my novel *A Passionate Hope: Hannah's Story*. One thing we do know is that she was the wife Elkanah loved, but she was denied her heart's desire for a son.

Have you ever asked God for something and received no answer? I think if we're honest, we all have to say yes.

I believe prayer is one of the most misunderstood and difficult things for Christians to do. We all know that we *should* pray. Read our Bibles and pray—these are the two main pillars that strengthen our faith.

I remember being taught these things from early childhood. Jesus meant everything to me, and I talked to Him like I would talk to a friend as I walked to and from school. In my youth group the leader would ask us to pray in a group setting. Out loud. We would all sit around a table waiting for someone to start. Nobody wanted to be that person, and there were very few who would risk praying so others could hear. I have a feeling the reason wasn't because we didn't ever pray, but we were more afraid of how to say the right words. We didn't want our friends to think we were weird or stupid if we tripped up.

Maybe that's because all we ever heard were those long pastoral prayers or prayers with big words from our leaders. Looking back, I can see what a difference it might have made to us if we had learned to understand prayer as a conversation that never ends. One where we knew we could come to God with anything. As Philippians 4:6–7 tells us,

> Don't worry about anything; instead, pray about everything; tell God your needs, and don't forget to thank him for his answers. If you do this, you will experience God's peace, which is far more wonderful than the human mind can understand. His peace will keep your thoughts and your hearts quiet and at rest as you trust in Christ Jesus. (TLB)

I was never taught honesty with God. I did learn to be honest with Him, but it came through much struggle on my part. How many of us are taught to tell God when we are thinking something that would offend every Christian we know? Or that we are engaging or want to engage in something we shouldn't? Or that we don't trust Him? Or that we are angry with Him because He isn't listening and isn't changing our circumstances when we know He can?

I think those kinds of prayers—those honest, heart-wrenching prayers—please God. He already knows our thoughts. He can tell us what we're going to say before we say it, so don't you think He knows what we're thinking?

I've had many wrestling-in-prayer matches with God. I've had my share of wondering if He cared, because He said to ask and we'd receive, and I ask but don't receive. I mean, doesn't the Bible say to ask, to keep asking, and God will answer? Especially if we are praying according to God's will? If we know from His Word that He desires the same things, why does He not give us a quick answer to our prayers?

In studying Scripture for many years, particularly the lives of people in the Old Testament, I've come to the conclusion that when Jesus said, "Ask and you will receive," He didn't tell us that there could be a long pause between those two verbs. But if you look at the lives of those ancient saints (and many current-day ones), you see that God often put "wait" between the promise and the receiving of it. Or between the request and the answer.

Abraham was promised a son. He waited twenty-five years to see that promise fulfilled (Gen. 13:14–16).

Isaac was that promised son who was to continue the line that would produce more offspring than the number of stars in the sky. Yet his wife remained barren for twenty years (Gen. 25:19, 26).

Joseph was given dreams of a future in which he would rule over his family. He spent twenty-two years away from them as a slave in Egypt before he saw that dream come true (Gen. 37:2; 41:46–47; 45:6).

Judah ran away from God's purpose for him and married a foreign woman. He returned to his family a changed man sometime before the famine hit that would reconcile him to his brother Joseph (Gen. 44:18–34).

Hannah prayed for a child for an untold number of years. God finally gave her Samuel and five more children after him (1 Sam. 1:20; 2:21).

Daniel prayed for understanding of a vision, and though God immediately heard his prayer, Daniel's spiritual enemies (demons) delayed the angel sent to answer him (Dan. 10:12–14).

Elijah prayed that it wouldn't rain, and it didn't for three years. When he prayed for rain to come again, he had to continue praying seven times before the cloud appeared in the sky (1 Kings 18:43–45).

Zechariah and Elizabeth prayed for a child so long, she was past her childbearing years. Then God decided to answer their prayers, which left Zechariah dumbstruck (Luke 1:5–25).

Paul prayed to be allowed to take the gospel to Asia, but God turned his path to Macedonia at that time instead (Acts 16:6–10).

Jesus said at the end of Revelation, "I am coming soon" (22:20). Over two thousand years later, "soon" is still in process.

So does this mean we stop asking? What happens to us as believers when we decide prayer isn't worth it because God doesn't care? What do we do with those times when we question God's character and wonder why bad things happen if He truly loves us? Why does evil—or, as in Hannah's day, corrupt and evil religious leaders—rule the day?

The Israelites knew that when evil gained the upper hand in their country, it had everything to do with the fact that they had turned their backs on worshiping God alone. Someone somewhere had turned to worshiping the idols of the people who lived near them. When God is no longer our God, prayer doesn't make sense. Why would we see a need for it?

Think of prayer like talking to someone you love—a spouse, a sibling, a parent, a child, or a friend. One day that person doesn't live up to your expectations, so you turn away from them. You cut them off or make new friends or get a divorce or some other type of separation. You stop talking. Other things or people take their place.

That's how it was for ancient Israel. That's how it is for us when we let other relationships or things take God's place. He didn't heal someone we prayed would get well. He didn't help us on the biggest test of our lives. He didn't stop that relative from hurting us. He didn't give us the desire of our heart. He hasn't led us to find the person we can love for a lifetime. He didn't give this blessing or stop that tragedy. He could have kept that plane from going down or those ships from colliding. He could have set up a different king or ruler of a nation—any nation. And we are stuck with evil rulers or corrupt businesspeople or a city that is falling down around us. So we turn away from God.

The list could go on and on. When God said to pray about everything, He meant it. That touches every area of our lives. So when we pray and God doesn't answer in the time we'd like, seeds of doubt in His character and ability take root. And it's oh so easy to forget the many times He's answered us in the past. The times He has said yes.

Do you have a gratitude journal? Do you keep track of the times God has said yes or answered you right away?

I've mentioned waiting twenty years to see my books in print. But God has also answered heartfelt prayers in sur-prisingly quick ways. One day, I was deeply burdened by something that was affecting one of our children. There was nothing I could do about it except pray. (That really ought to be the first thing we do, but we tend to think of it as our last resort.) I hopped on the treadmill, back in the days when I used it faithfully, and I walked and I prayed. I sought God for the situation with this child. I could see it going in the wrong direction but couldn't see a way to fix it. So I asked God to do so.

When I finished praying, nothing happened except that I had placed it in His hands. Two days later, circumstances changed such that I knew God had answered my prayer. He had done so in a way I could not have imagined and would not have chosen. It was all God.

I'm still praying for things that have gone on for years. I can't control these circumstances either, but I figure if God could answer so surprisingly and rather amazingly back then, He can do the same again in the future. I'm just caught between the now and the not yet.

Have you been there? Have you been asking God for something and feel as though He has not heard? Are you discouraged, as Hannah surely was, that other people seem to be getting their hearts' desires but you are denied?

I suspect Hannah felt differently after one final, all-out, desperate prayer.

## Imagine with Me

It has always been hard for me to stop hoping. Oh, I have come close many times, but there is something inside of me that can't give up. I suppose that is a good quality to have. I can't give up on a stubborn knot in the weaving or a weed that fights me when I attempt to dig it up. I don't even truly give up on people, though Hophni and Phineas and Peninnah have all given me good reason to.

Elkanah tells me he admires my spirit, but he doesn't see that I'm just stubborn. Yet even stubborn people can lose heart. And that last feast when Peninnah simply would not stop taunting me . . . I could bear no more. Elkanah cannot understand. He thinks he should be enough for me, but to watch *her* with her sons and daughters surrounding her, while I am given extra meat, as if that should satisfy . . .

I stumble away from the feast and make my way to the tabernacle. I have to pray. I cannot run home to the woods to pray or stray far with so many people surrounding the tabernacle. So I walk, barely able to hold myself upright, to the place where the corrupt priests hold sway, where their father, Eli, watches over the holy things.

Tears fall like hot embers over my cheeks, and I crumble to the dirt near the tabernacle, as close as I am allowed to go.

*O Lord of Heaven's Armies, if You will look upon my sorrow and answer my prayer and give me a son, then I will give him back to You. He will be Yours for his entire lifetime, and as a sign that he has been dedicated to the Lord, his hair will never be cut.*

More words pour from my heart, and my lips move, but I cannot speak aloud. Never have I offered such a prayer. To give such a vow is not something I take lightly. I have thought often to pray thus, but until tonight I could never bring myself to that point. To give back what is given . . . But I know this is the exact prayer God hears, and even through my tears, I sense peace.

Eli sees me and thinks me a drunken woman, but once he understands the truth, he blesses me. How light my heart feels all of a sudden.

Surely I surrendered my will to God's before now, but still I had no assurance that He had heard my quiet pleas. Now, however . . . now I am filled with joy. I cannot hold back the smile that carries me through the camp to our tent. Elkanah notices. He worries overmuch about me. There is no need to worry any longer.

Now I know. The truth is that God does hear our prayers. I suspect He has heard every one that I have prayed since my youth. But sometimes He delays His answers for a season. Only He knows why.

The only thing I know, after giving Him my heart and promising to dedicate His gift back to Him, is that He is going to give me the child for whom I prayed. I do not know when. But I know it will be soon. And that knowledge fills me with such joy. I cannot stop smiling.

## From Despair to Joy

If you read Hannah's story in 1 Samuel, you get a glimpse of what her life was like. She shared her husband with a sister-wife. Since Hannah's name is listed first, my guess is that she was his first wife. Peninnah may have come along to give him sons because of Hannah's barrenness.

The Bible tells us,

> So Peninnah would taunt Hannah and make fun of her because the LORD had kept her from having children. Year after year it was the same—Peninnah would taunt Hannah as they went to the Tabernacle. Each time, Hannah would be reduced to tears and would not even eat. (1 Sam. 1:6–7 NLT)

I cannot imagine any scenario where that would be a pleasant household, can you? Polygamy can get people into all kinds of trouble, but that's not our main concern here. The problem was that Hannah's life was miserable and there was nothing she could do about it.

There are so many ways we can imagine misery. Those of us who have lived with abuse, have been raped, suffer from PTSD, have mental issues, are addicted to a substance or a harmful behavior—whatever it may be, our circumstances can destroy us or make us stronger.

Hannah chose to seek the Lord and relied on Him, and it made her a stronger, sweeter, better woman in the process. Not everyone has the same outcome. We all know people—or perhaps we are those people—who become bitter, reclusive, angry, or basically unhappy. Even Christians can fall into these categories. It's so easy to do. Some of it has to do with our personality. Some of it has to do with the circumstances of our childhood. Some of it has to do with our own choices. The truth is we are responsible for whether we will remain in despair or seek joy.

But in that despair or joy, a big component of our choice will be whether or not we give up on God. I know that sounds impossible for a Christian, but it's not. Many people who once truly loved Him grow disillusioned or disappointed with life. And when that happens, we tend to blame God for not making life better for us. After all, wasn't that supposed to be part of the blessing of becoming a Christian in the first place? God would supply all of our needs. He would give us our heart's desires. He made promises we haven't seen Him keep, so why should we keep asking, keep waiting? Why not give up on God?

If Hannah could speak to us today, I think she could tell us why not. She would lift up her squalling son and show us the answer to her prayers. And she would tell us that the wait was worth it. That the taunts of her sister-wife mean nothing to her now. That God has filled her heart with joy. The song she sang after taking Samuel to live at the tabernacle mimics Mary's Magnificat in Luke 1:

> My heart rejoices in the LORD!
> The LORD has made me strong.
> Now I have an answer for my enemies;
> I rejoice because you rescued me.

No one is holy like the LORD!
There is no one besides you;
there is no Rock like our God. (1 Sam. 2:1–2 NLT)

God tells us to pray and not give up. In essence, that means He doesn't want us to give up on Him or to lose heart. He wants us to be courageous in prayer even when we don't see Him working. Even if we wonder if He hears us. Even though we don't get the answer we ask for right away. Even if we get a different answer, which turns out to be the best answer in the end.

I remember when we were looking for a new house. We found one we thought would be great for our growing family, so we put an offer on it, contingent on us selling our smaller ranch. We worked like crazy to fix up our old house, but after two months, the other house sold out from under us.

I was devastated. The problem was that we couldn't find another house that came close to what we wanted. My husband didn't give up looking, but I did. I determined to be at peace with where we were. We would remodel and make two bedrooms work for the three kids we wanted.

Then one day Randy came home and said he'd found a house three blocks away that was for sale by owner. It was a fixer-upper, but it was the layout we wanted. So I went with him to see it.

The house was truly a disaster. Though structurally sound, it had so many things wrong. It needed nearly everything updated, like the kitchen and bathrooms and paint and carpet and on and on. But we decided to put in another contingent offer and put our house up for sale by owner too.

Weeks went by, and I began to lose heart. We were obviously meant to stay where we were. Until one day our house sold, and we bought that fixer-upper, which we are now fixing up again in preparation to sell—thirty years later!

To say it was a great house would be a lie. I would walk in and clean, then go home and cry. (I didn't know I was pregnant, which didn't help my emotions.) The former owners had raised eight boys in the house, and trust me when I say it needed a super cleaning. I cleaned the toilets four times before I would use one!

But now I look back and think that this was the better house. The better neighborhood in which to raise our sons. And for thirty years we've enjoyed this place, making it almost everything we imagined it could be.

Unfortunately, life has a way of slipping by when we aren't looking, and now we find ourselves in that same place of wanting to move. This house is too big for two people, and it's not a good idea to have stairs as we get older. There are a lot of other reasons I want to go, but so far, God hasn't said where or when. We pray, but we also wait. As with the other house, we will know when it's God's time. And hopefully, the next place won't need much fixing, because we're not as energetic as we were back then.

Whether our prayers are for things like where to live or who to marry or how to mend a broken world, we can't give up and think God's not listening. He cares about that messed-up marriage or that hurting child. He cares about the homeless and the refugees, people caught in human trafficking and in evil regimes, and those who are persecuted for their faith.

God loves us. He doesn't withhold His answers because He's trying to be mean. He didn't keep Hannah from having a child out of cruelty or to watch her suffer. We will never know His reasons, because they are so far above our thinking.

God is both knowable and unknowable. He reveals much about Himself in Scripture, and He keeps much from us as well. The finite cannot truly comprehend the choices of the infinite.

But we can obey Him. And He tells us to pray and not give up. To keep praying, keep asking, keep seeking, keep knocking. Hannah did, and God gave her a longed-for son.

There is hope in the waiting if we don't lose heart.

## Ponder This

Prayer is not something we do so we can check it off our spiritual growth chart. It is not something we do to be seen by others so we're thought of as a good Christian. Prayer is conversation between a holy God and His people. He invites us into that conversation and gives us guidelines, such as remembering who He is, thanking Him for what He's already done, and asking Him to meet our needs—to feed us, to keep us from temptation, to deliver us from evil. He wants us to pray about everything.

Tell God your needs, and don't forget to thank him for his answers. (Phil. 4:6 TLB)

Jesus encouraged His disciples to pray and not give up. The first line of defense against sin, against the flesh that pulls us away from God, and against despair is to pray. It doesn't matter whether we are on our knees or walking along the road or running a race or sitting in a hospital bed. Wherever we are, God is listening. He is everywhere. And if we seek Him with all of our hearts, we will find Him.

## TAKING IT FURTHER

1. Have you ever gotten so discouraged with life that you gave up praying because you didn't think it did any good? How did that distance from God make you feel?

2. Do you believe that God hears you when you pray? If so, how does that make a difference in the way you converse with Him? Is prayer more of a duty or more like breathing—something you couldn't live without? Explain your answer.

3. If you have given up on God, how can you turn around and see things differently? Considering Hannah didn't give up on God, how does her example help you?

# Peninnah

## When Hurt and Hate Are All You Feel

*(Based on 1 Samuel 1–2)*

### If I Were Peninnah

I crawl out of bed, a bed I rarely share with my husband, and force myself to answer the cry of my youngest son. If I don't shush him quickly, he will wake the other children, and I have no energy to deal with them yet.

I snatch Nadav from his small bed beside me and put him to my breast, but there is no joy in nursing him as there had been with his brothers and sisters. I am weary of bearing children, though I will never let Hannah know that. To the one who has no child but owns my husband's heart, I flaunt every son and daughter. She needs to see that she is not better than I. I have value, am of *more* value to Elkanah than she is. Without me, he would have no sons.

My son's mouth tugs hard and he nearly bites, though he has no teeth. I cry out and hold him back. He wails. I give in and let him suckle.

I hate my life.

I wish I had never married Elkanah. People told me I could never win his love away from Hannah. I did not believe them. Even with the birth of six children, he still barely looks my way. Even my sons betray me when they want to spend time with her.

I wish I had never been born. Then I would not have had to live to see that I am not wanted or appreciated. If I were, perhaps the constant ache in my heart would go away. Even if I cannot have his love, it would help to know he wants me. Is glad of the sons and daughters I have given to him.

Instead, when I go through the agony of birth, he goes off to find *her*, afraid that she is sad because we are celebrating. Who should care what she is feeling? Hannah is worthless. Barren. And Elkanah should have put her out long ago. Sent her back to her father.

But no. He clings to her more each year. He showers her with gifts, takes her to Shiloh when he goes to work there, and lets her join him in the fields when he tends the sheep. He would have had my sons call her Ima Hannah if I had not put a stop to it.

My son finally sleeps, and I release a deep sigh. My head slumps against the cushion, and I feel the prick of angry tears. Why do I feel no joy in this child's birth? The others had distracted me for a time until they all grew so demanding. Parenting them on my own without Elkanah's help or the help of his family—they all hate me—is impossible. I cannot bear it.

My mother told me to make Hannah bitter. Then she would complain to Elkanah and he would turn to me instead. But nothing I say or do has helped. Instead, Elkanah's family defends her! Nobody cares for me. No one loves me, not even these awful children.

I lay my son back in his bed and curl into a ball, allowing the tears to wet the linen beneath me. I hate my life.

I wish I had never been born.

## What We Know

I know my imagination of Peninnah's point of view sounds pretty bleak, and we cannot know for sure what she might have thought. We do know that she was Hannah's rival and constantly taunted her regarding her barrenness. We also know that she gave Elkanah many sons and daughters. But have you ever wondered what her life might have been like to make her so mean? Was she a bully as a young girl? I know *bully* is a modern term, but mean girls and boys have existed since Adam and Eve. Remember Cain and Abel? If one brother can kill another near the beginning of recorded history, we know sin has been with us for a very long time.

Cruelty among the young is nothing new. Teachers see it in their classrooms. Fights break out in schools over social media comments or the way one person looks at another. I hear about such things over our dinner conversation, so I know they happen.

I would classify Peninnah as a bully to Hannah. A grown-up one, but a bully nonetheless. What made her that way? Those are the questions I like to ask when I write about a person in Scripture, or even when I'm trying to understand a friend's behavior.

People are complex, but in many ways we are not as unique as we'd like to think. Jesus understands that about us. The apostle John tells us of a time when Jesus did a lot of miracles during the Passover in Jerusalem, and because of them, many people began to trust in Him. Then John says, "But Jesus didn't trust them, because he knew all about people. No one needed to tell him about human nature, for he knew what was in each person's heart" (John 2:24–25 NLT).

Jesus knows how easy it is for us to harbor hurt or anger in our hearts. Peninnah was an angry person, and anger often comes from hurt. Hate does too, because when we're hurt or angry with someone, bitterness can form inside of us and, left unchecked, can grow to hatred.

When we turn anger inward, we become depressed and tend to take out our anger on ourselves. Thus Peninnah's thoughts above of hating her life and wishing she had never been born. Have you ever felt that way?

I think intense people might feel this way more than their easygoing counterparts do. People who feel strongly can go from love to hate in an instant. Or perhaps a week. The ancient Jews loved Jesus one day, and a week later they demanded His crucifixion. People are definitely fickle.

When we are hurting in the deep places in our soul, we want someone to notice. We want someone to care about us. We want hope, and we want to be loved. When we don't get that, we can be like Leah in Genesis and learn to let God be our heart's desire, or we can be like Peninnah and turn on everyone around us and grow into a bitter person. There really are no other choices. We have to do something with our hurt and anger, and if we hold on to the anger, it's going to either explode all over the people around us or turn inward until we want to die.

Unless a person has a mental illness or struggles to control their emotions for some physical reason, happiness is something we can choose. I learned a lot about happiness many years ago. I discovered that often when we feel depressed or guilty, we can trace those feelings to anger turned inward. Since I've felt both depressed and guilty at times, I decided to practice searching for the anger or fear that could be the root of the problem. In addition to prayer, it helps to search my heart for hurt or anger or some other emotion that might be causing my depression or guilt or even anxiety. When I do so, I can usually find the reason. Maybe I'm upset because someone said they were going to do something and then didn't. Or maybe I expected a situation or event to go a certain way and it didn't. Sometimes it really does help to keep our expectations low.

Maybe that's why Jesus didn't trust people. He knew what was in human nature. But trust has nothing to do with His love for us. He absolutely, unconditionally loves people. He died because of love. But He didn't trust people because He knew we would break our word. (His disciples all promised to go with him to death and then deserted him.) He knew we wouldn't do what He asked us to. (He healed a leper and told him not to tell anyone but to show himself to the priest as the law required, and the man went and spread the word far and wide anyway.) He knew we would fail Him, deny Him, run from Him, desert Him, betray Him, and even hate Him.

Would you trust us if you were Him?

So Jesus knew what was in the hearts of people, including Peninnah's. He knew why she bullied Hannah. He saw Hannah's suffering, but He also saw Peninnah's.

God loved Peninnah as much as He did Hannah.

Bitter people like Peninnah take their hurt and anger out on other people. They don't turn to God for help with that hurt like Hannah did. But that didn't stop God from loving Peninnah. He created all of us. Whether we choose to love and trust in Him or become bitter and stay away from Him, we will not lose His love. We might lose a relationship we could have had, but God still loves the whole world.

The whole world, however, does not love God in return. And that's where we find Peninnah living in her unhappy circumstances.

## Imagine with Me

I heard her singing. Hateful woman. I know she aimed those words—"the woman with many children wastes away"—at me. She does not know that. I'm not wasting away! I'm young and strong and can bear many more sons for Elkanah. Just because she has *one* son and gave him to live at the tabernacle doesn't mean she's better than I.

I think she's worse. What mother could give up her child to live with that old man, Eli? Worse, what caring woman would want her son to live near those awful sons of Eli?

Elkanah must be made to see that what Hannah has done is reprehensible. She made a vow, she said. Then she sang a song and praised the Lord after Samuel left us. It makes no sense.

She probably also thought of me when she said, "Stop acting so proud and haughty! Don't speak with such arrogance! For the Lord is a God who knows what you have done. He will judge your actions."

I haven't done anything worth judging. If anything, it is *I* who have done well for Elkanah. I came into his barren home and gave him a family. I have sacrificed for him and put up with her for years, but what praise does he lavish on me? What do I get for it?

Nothing. I hope she is happy now that she is childless again. Oh, she will go to visit her son, but will she have another? She's growing old. Soon it will be too late for her to bear.

Laughter rises from within me, and I cannot help but give in to its bitter clatter against my ears.

I turn at the sound of my children playing in the yard. Their laughter is happy, free. I used to feel that way once. When I was young and the only child of my mother. When I had no cares but to do as I pleased. When I didn't care if a man loved me or not.

Perhaps that is the source of all my pain. I care too much. But how can I not? I want Elkanah. To myself. I want Hannah gone.

I will never be happy until then.

## From Hate to Resignation

Hannah's song in Scripture uses the words that I had Peninnah thinking. Whether Hannah aimed them at her rival, only God knows. But as I wrote Hannah's story, those chosen words of praise—which moved on to speak of pride, arrogance, the barren woman, and the woman with children—seemed to have a reason for being.

We never hear of Peninnah again after this incident in 1 Samuel. Her whole life's story in Scripture seems to teach us what not to be. I must say, though, that I have a small sense of compassion for Peninnah, simply because I don't know what made her the way she was.

I've watched couples in love stand at the altar and vow to cherish each other until death parts them. I've said those words myself. Yet I've seen couples years later breaking those vows because of one reason or another. When I was growing up, divorce wasn't as popular as it is today. No-fault divorce (is that anything like no-fault insurance?) wasn't a thing in Michigan. But it was in another state. To take advantage of it, a family I knew moved to the state that offered it. I don't know if the wife knew the reason for moving there, but the man did. He wanted a divorce, and he didn't have a good reason. No-fault divorce allowed him to get what he wanted without having to give the judge an explanation.

The point is, while God's love never fails, human love can and does. It will never come close to the kind of love God has for us. For myself as a mom, that seems almost impossible because I don't know any mom who doesn't love her own kids with passion, no matter how old they get or what they do or say. Moms love. It's how we're wired.

But God's love? It's *way* beyond what we could imagine. We cannot even fathom it. Leah discovered that God had to be all she needed because she didn't have Jacob in the way she thought she needed him. Peninnah does not appear to have looked for love from God. She remained jealous and angry, as far as we know, for the rest of her life.

Just as I've seen couples in love declare their undying affection for their spouse, I've also seen bitter people destroy their own lives and the lives of those around them. Bitter people ruin their own health, their relationships, their goals and dreams, even their very souls.

If Peninnah thought her children could make up for Elkanah's love, she didn't show it. The truth is, they couldn't. They grew up and moved on to marry and have families of their own. Some cultures live with extended family, and Peninnah probably did too. But chances are she didn't find the happiness she was seeking even there, because only God could have given her what she desired. Only God could replace the anger and hurt with joy and gladness. Instead of resigning herself to continue in her hatred, she could have surrendered it and asked God for His love. But she would have had to put aside that pride and arrogance Hannah spoke of in her song.

We don't do that very easily, do we? To find the love of God filling our hearts, we have to surrender the pride of our hearts to Him. That means being humble and forgiving and seeking forgiveness, and those are hard for all of us, not just the bullies among us.

My grandfather used to sing a song in prisons (as a visitor, not a prisoner) and probably sang it in churches too. I think he even recorded the song on a record, though I'm not sure where that record has gone. The words are beautiful, and I thought I would share them, as they help describe God's love better than I can.

> The love of God is greater far
> than tongue or pen can ever tell;
> it goes beyond the highest star,
> and reaches to the lowest hell.
> The guilty pair, bowed down with care,
> God gave his Son to win;
> his erring child he reconciled,
> and pardoned from his sin.
>
> Could we with ink the ocean fill,
> and were the skies of parchment made;
> were every stalk on earth a quill,
> and every man a scribe by trade;
> to write the love of God above
> would drain the ocean dry;
> nor could the scroll contain the whole,
> though stretched from sky to sky.

O love of God, how rich and pure;
how measureless and strong!
It shall forevermore endure,
the saints' and angels' song.

Frederick M. Lehman,
"The Love of God"


## Ponder This

None of us are going to live a perfectly happy life. Not here. This earth is broken, and our hearts . . . well, Jesus knows what is in our hearts. And if we examine them, we know too, don't we? As I have learned how to search for anger or fear when I have depression or guilt, so we can learn to ask God to show us anything that keeps us from the joy of knowing Him. We can let His love fill our hearts instead of becoming controlled by bitterness.

When we think God doesn't care or isn't listening, let's not be like Peninnah but remember Hannah's song instead:

He raises up the poor from the dust;
   he lifts the needy from the ash heap
to make them sit with princes
   and inherit a seat of honor.
For the pillars of the earth are the LORD's,
   and on them he has set the world. (1 Sam. 2:8)

Our Creator controls this world, and He loves each and every one of us, even if we've acted like a bully. It is never too late to give our hurt and anger and bitterness and fear to Him. We don't have to end up like Peninnah. We are God's beloved. There is no one like our God.

## TAKING IT FURTHER

1. Has there been a time in your life when you've been so hurt and angry that you allowed it to make you bitter? How did you handle those feelings? Are you still dealing with them, or have you learned to give them to God?

2. Have you ever been bullied by a bitter person? Can you describe the incident? What did you do to stop the bully from attacking you, and what did you learn from that?

3. Do you think giving up your hurts and your bitterness is an easy decision? Why or why not?

# Michal

## Finding the Life You Lost

*(Based on 1 Samuel 18:17—19:17; 2 Samuel 6:16—23)*

### If I Were Michal

The light from the window fades in and out, though they tell me the sun still sits high in the sky. No clouds mar the blue of the heavens, they say, but here where I lie among the rich cushions in the king's palace near my window, I do not see them.

I didn't expect to miss my sight so much, but everything around me grows dim. Time—ah, how it changes things. Long ago, life as a king's daughter was never dull. My father made sure of that. Too often Abba's thoughts sent him into a rage, and David came to play his harp for him.

I fell in love with David in those first few visits. How well I remember! The love I had for him consumed me, and I did everything in my power to convince my father that David should belong to me.

So much has changed.

I turn at the sound of a young maid, whose name I no longer remember. I see the outline of youth in her form.

"Is there anything I can get for you, my queen?"

"I am not your queen." At least I can still speak, though the girl bends closer as though my words are hard to hear. Who exactly is growing old?

I shake my head. I am not hungry or thirsty and have little energy to rise today. Perhaps tomorrow things will be different.

When did my life become so mundane?

My thoughts drift again, and in my mind's eye I see Jonathan and David discussing plans for war in our sitting room. Once again Jonathan is telling us that our father is going to kill David. I never thought helping David run off like that would mean I would lose him. How many years were lost until my whole family was dead and he ruled all of Israel?

I close my eyes, though I no longer feel emotion over their loss. I don't even care for or miss Paltiel, the man my father forced me to marry in David's place. The girl who once tried to control her world slipped away when she lost everything.

The servant returns a few moments later and helps me to sit, though I did not ask it of her. I blink, trying better to see my surroundings. Things blur before my eyes now, and I do not enjoy the taste of the food I once loved. I still hear clearly, so I suppose I can be grateful for that.

If I have any regrets in my long years on earth, they would be that David and I were parted and that I tried too hard to control everyone around me. If I hadn't begged for David's hand in marriage, if I hadn't convinced Father to give Merab to Adriel, if I hadn't lied to save David's life and been forced to marry Paltiel, if I'd been able to run from him and join David in exile, then perhaps . . . well, life would have been so much better. Or at least different. If only there would have been a way for me to have stayed with my husband instead of under my father's control.

Would I have truly changed who I was back then? If anything, I would have tried harder to stop what was done to me. But I had no control over any of that. I can say I am grateful that at last I did make peace with David. He does not love me like he loved me then, but he no longer stays away.

A knock on the door makes me turn, and I wait among the cushions of my sitting room, dressed now and grateful for the warmth of the sun when it angles across my knees through the windows. I can hear conversation in the hall, and moments later, as if my memories have produced him, David moves into the room and takes the seat opposite me.

"Good day to you, Michal." His voice still carries a melodic sound.

"My lord king." I bow slightly, then lift my head, squinting to better see his face. "How may I help you?" It is not like him to visit often, but when he does, I still feel a little kick in my heart.

"You may stay where you are and let me enjoy your company." He leans closer and takes my hand. His is warm compared to mine. "I have been meaning to come sooner. How have you been feeling?"

I chuckle. "Are they telling you I am ill? I am younger than you are, David. I am simply having trouble seeing as well as I used to. But I am not ill."

"And you are eating enough?"

How I wish I could read the expression in those dark, reflective eyes!

"Do you have spies watching my every move?" I smile, warmed by his concern. Something he did not have for many years. How blessed I feel to know that God has restored at least in part the many years that were stolen from us.

David laughs at my comment, drawing me back to the present. "They update me on many things, my love. And I am told you are not eating enough."

I make a face and wave a hand as though to bat his words away. "They know nothing. I eat when I'm hungry. I only wish I could see to do the things I once loved."

He grows silent a moment. "As do I." His voice sounds distant. He turns my hand over in his and interlaces our fingers. "Whatever you need, you have only to ask. Have the servants take you on walks through the gardens. The fresh air will do you good. And I would enjoy seeing you at the meals now and then."

"You would have me sit with the women of your house?" He has kept me from him for so long that this surprises me. I've grown used to eating alone and mostly prefer it that way.

"If you can tolerate her, Bathsheba would enjoy your company. You and she are among the few of my wives who still live, other than Haggith and the concubines." There is regret in his tone, and I know he probably misses Abigail most of all. Will he miss me as much when I go the way of all the earth?

"I've always liked Bathsheba," I say, though I'm not sure that is the whole truth. "At least, I have come to enjoy her company in the past few years."

"Then it is settled. You must join her tonight and listen to the music and the conversation, even if you cannot see the dancers and jugglers as you once did." He pauses, and I hear him sigh. "I wish things had been different for you, Michal."

Is he thinking of the child I lost? Or the rest of my family who died in war or to pay off a debt? It matters little. He has lost nearly as much as I have, though he still has children.

"I wish so too, David." My words are hushed, and I hope he hears them. "But we cannot change what God has willed. We can only live with the time we have left and do our best to please Him."

"How you have changed," he says, and there is pleasure in his voice. "I'm glad you have made your peace with Him."

"And I'm glad you have made your peace with me." My words are barely a whisper. "We have both suffered much and learned much. But I suppose it is in losing that we often find what has been missing and gain more than we expected."

He seems to ponder my words, and we sit in companionable silence for a moment. "Yes," he says at last. "Perhaps we needed to be apart in order to appreciate each other. We have both learned from what we have lost. And been forgiven. It is a great gift of grace that God has allowed us that." He stands and leans close to kiss my cheek. "I will see you tonight at the evening meal then."

I nod. "I will be there."

"Good."

I squeeze his hand and release it, then listen as he walks away. The door closes behind him, and I sit for a time reflecting on the past and on what has passed between us. I would change a lot of things if I had life to live over again. But I would not change what life with David has taught me. What God has taught me through each new situation.

None of my life has truly been mine to control. In my youth I only thought it was. Now, as time dulls my vision, I actually see more clearly than I did back then. I see as one to whom

God has given new insight. And I would not go back or change anything for that.

## What We Know

Michal's story is a tragic one in Scripture. Though she was likely considered a princess during her father's reign as king, she was the youngest child and lived to see the loss of every sibling and both parents, as well as her uncle and five nephews. While she may have gotten her way in her desire to marry David, that desire was short-lived, and she was given to another man in marriage. Hardly the ideal life.

Though she couldn't control her world—none of us can—I see Michal as one who wanted just that. But she was not powerful enough to make anything happen the way she envisioned.

Even though control is an illusion, that doesn't stop us from trying to control our circumstances. I think loss increases our desire to do so. When we lose one thing, we tend to fear losing another. Fear can lead us into control-freak behavior.

You've seen it in those around you, haven't you? Perhaps you've even seen it in yourself. I know I have. And lately, I've discovered more clearly how it has been handed down in the family—not just my family but families in every generation.

I think of my grandmother, whom I dearly loved. When I was small, she used to babysit me while my mom worked. She would pull out her box of pictures and tell me the stories behind them. One particular photo and accompanying story has stayed with me as a rather sad tale, and it changed the way my grandmother viewed her world for the rest of her life.

The picture was of her and her sister, who were the youngest of five girls and one boy. My grandma and her sister were both holding dolls. They seemed happy. But Grandma went on to tell me that they were only allowed to keep those dolls for one year. Then their mother made them give the dolls to their older brother's children.

As I had lunch with my mom the other day, I asked her questions about my grandma. We commented on Grandma's controlling nature, and I wondered what had made her that way. The attitude of only keeping things for a year came up, and I learned that my mom and her sister were also only allowed to keep their dolls for a year. (In contrast, I still have my baby doll, though it's time to let her go.)

My great-grandmother's forcing her young daughters to give up their only real possessions after a year made a huge impact on my grandmother. She never kept anything that she didn't use more than a year. If she had two coats, she gave one away. My mom learned to do the same, though she didn't force that on me. And she didn't carry the hurt of giving things away that my grandma seemed to carry.

Loss affects each one of us differently. Until that conversation with my mom, I never realized how much loss could change a person's outlook on life. Maybe my grandma just didn't think we should cling to earthly things, and if what we have could benefit someone else, then we should give freely. That's not a bad lesson to learn.

But loss can also lead us to cling tightly to things that are not ours to keep or control. Maybe it's a small thing, like not wanting anyone to help you when you are putting on a sumptuous meal because you want it to be perfect and don't trust anyone else. Or maybe it goes deeper than that, like not wanting anyone else to teach your child, not even at church or school or outside classes, because you don't want them to learn from anyone but you. (Side note: I'm not dissing homeschooling.

I homeschooled my children for twelve years. But I still involved them in many outside opportunities to learn from other people, whether in a gym class or on a sports team or in church or in anything they wanted to do.) We can't cut ourselves off from the world. It has a way of creeping in whether we want it to or not.

Control, like the kind Michal's father held over her, hurts people. Her father, King Saul, was told God had torn the kingdom from him and was going to give it to another, but he would not go silently into the night. He fought to keep his rule. For a man who started out with humble beginnings, he turned into a man who took charge of things that weren't his to do—like offering a sacrifice that only priests were allowed to offer, or building a monument to himself after a war he'd won. Except he didn't complete that war according to God's commands. Saul grew increasingly paranoid and tried relentlessly to kill David, his own son-in-law, and in the end consulted a medium instead of the Lord. The mighty king had fallen and fallen hard.

And he was Michal's example. She'd grown up watching him rule, lived with his bouts of insanity, and later heard her brothers had died in battle beside him. Years later, after she'd been taken from David and then returned to him, she despised David's worship of the Lord and publicly condemned him for it. In a sense, her losses, or perhaps the example she grew up with, had led her to act much like her father.

The Bible doesn't tell us if there was a good outcome to Michal's life. It ends with the fact that she had no children. We can leave it there and assume the worst of her, or we can see the possibility of change in the end. I like to imagine that Michal had a better ending and that we just don't know the full story.

## Imagine with Me

The sun no longer warms me as I walk with my maid among the gardens. I no longer know the different maids who take turns watching over me, but I hold on to their arms so they can guide my way as I breathe in the scent of almond blossoms and picture the beauty they hold this time of year.

I wonder what life would have been like if my father had never been made king all those years ago. He hadn't sought the position. God had chosen him because the people demanded a king. I was barely old enough to know my own mind when he came to power. I wish that day had not been. I think life in the fields of Grandfather Kish would have been happier than the days in a fortress and our men rushing off to constant war.

Perhaps Merab and I would have gotten along sooner if we hadn't been in competition for David's hand. I know I hurt her by scheming to have her given to someone else. Shame briefly heats my face at the memory, but I know Merab forgave me long ago. She had a good life with Adriel.

The breeze tickles the back of my neck, and a slight shiver moves through me. "Perhaps we should go inside." I turn toward the maid who holds my arm, and she turns us toward the palace. I do not handle the cold as I once did.

As we reach the door, I pause a moment and lift my gaze heavenward. I can barely feel the sun or see the stars, but I can feel that the presence of God is near. As though He sees me and is as close as my breath.

Even with all of my failures and bitter words and gigantic losses, I am filled with gratitude. I know now that when God chose my father to be king, He chose our family to be in the place we were meant to be. It was up to each of us whether or not we were going to trust Him.

Jonathan trusted God best. I wish I had learned that lesson from him far sooner than I did. I think the turbulence of my life kept me focused too much on myself, and I had no use for the God of our people.

Until I desperately needed Him. And in that moment, He came to me and blessed me with forgiveness and restored relationships. No matter how long I live, those things will always mean more to me than anything I have lost. My hope and joy have been found.

## From Loss to Gain

As I've pointed out, Michal suffered the physical loss of everyone in her family except for David, and she lost her relationship with him as well. As far as we know, she may never have regained that. We can only hope.

Have you ever experienced devastating loss? What did that do to your emotions, your overall outlook on life?

We are all going to face loss at some time in our lives, but the bigger question comes in how we react to it. Can loss like Michal dealt with bring ultimate gain?

Jesus said, "For whoever would save his life will lose it, but whoever loses his life for my sake will find it. For what will it profit a man if he gains the whole world and forfeits his soul? Or what shall a man give in return for his soul?" (Matt. 16:25–26).

Some losses in this life bring far greater gains in the next one. If Michal had not grown bitter, perhaps she would not have berated David for worshiping God in a way that didn't meet her standards. She might have realized that bitterness would only hurt herself and the people who cared about her the most. Might she have confessed that bitterness to the

Lord and been healed? I hope so. Even if her relationship with David was never healed, she could have certainly known God's forgiveness if she but asked.

Isn't that how life is for all of us? Whether we suffer a financial, physical, health, or relational loss, each has the potential to teach us to lay aside our control of this life, live for the Lord, and enjoy His grace in the next life. Or we can remain bitter and unchanged and lose even more than we already have.

My grandmother chose to seek forgiveness from those she had tried to control. And when she died, the last word on her lips was "Jesus."

I'd like to think that Michal is waiting in heaven as one of those many witnesses mentioned in Hebrews 12:1. I'd like to think that unlike her father, she made peace with God.

One thing is certain. Either we can go from loss to gain, or we can remain in a state of bitterness and confusion and cling to what we can't get back and can't control. I hope each of us chooses to seek the gain of knowing Christ rather than suffer the loss of all we hold dear.

## Ponder This

God understands what it feels like to lose those He loves. He suffered more than anyone can imagine when He sent His Son to die on the cross for us. *For us.* People who would rather gain the whole world and lose their own souls. That's not just some random person. That's you and me. We are all bent on heading in that direction if not for the grace of God. We can all end up like Michal's father and go from humble beginnings to paranoid control freaks.

Or we can be like those who refuse to chase after worldly things or cling to what is past, and instead embrace grace and turn from the things we try to control. Turn from the things that make us bitter. Surrender to the love that God wants so much to show us.

> For whoever would save his life will lose it, but whoever loses his life for my sake will find it. (Matt. 16:25)

> For God so loved the world, that he gave his only Son, that whoever believes in him should not perish but have eternal life. (John 3:16)

There is a one-letter difference between *lose* and *love*. When we lose our lives for the sake of following Jesus, we gain the love of God both in this life and for eternity. I would say that exchange is worth everything.

## TAKING IT FURTHER

1. How has loss affected your life? In what way has it changed your perspective? What would you tell someone who is facing loss right now?

2. When Jesus said it was better to lose your life for His sake than to keep it in an attempt to gain everything the world has to offer, what does that mean to you? Have you been in a place where you were willing to surrender your life for His sake rather than try to save what you cannot keep here?

3. Do you think Michal's life could have ended in a positive way, even though she never had children? Might she have had a change of heart toward God? Toward David? If not, how would her continued bitterness make you feel about her? About yourself?

# Abigail

## Wisdom to Appease

*(Based on 1 Samuel 25)*

### If I Were Abigail

The fields are ripe, the grain nearly ready to harvest. Nabal will expect me to keep accurate records of all that he puts in his ever-burgeoning barns. He expects me to keep accurate records of every morsel of food, be it raisin cakes, wine, olive oil, or kernels of grain, as if I'm supposed to count them one by one.

I manage to appease him. I've learned to count by bushels and can tell him how much yield a bushel will bring or what price it will give him at the market. As long as he isn't drinking and can be appeased, I am safe. And if I can keep him from my bed, so much the better.

The thought saddens me, for I had hoped my life would be so much different than this. When my father chose Nabal to be my husband, I never imagined what my life would become. What I would endure. I thought he would care for me as my father cared for my mother. I thought we would have children and be known as those who help others in the community.

I didn't expect to want to hide from those very people. But when Nabal is drunk and surly, or on those occasions when he has taken his rage out on me . . .

I turn back toward the house. To dwell on these things is depressing, and I will not allow Nabal to ruin my life. I will appease him any way I can, but I will keep my distance as well.

The sound of running feet causes me to turn toward the fields again. Nabal has been shearing sheep, and he and his men are about to begin celebrating his great wealth and the money he will make from the sale of the wool. But Nabal would not run, and the feet are those of a lighter man. I squint to see him.

One of Nabal's young men races toward me. He stops, hands on his knees, drawing breath. "Mistress Abigail."

"Yes? Tell me—what's wrong?" Has something happened to Nabal?

The man, not much more than a boy, looks up at me. "David sent messengers from the wilderness to greet our master, but he screamed insults at them. These men have been very good to us, and we never suffered any harm from them. Nothing was stolen from us the whole time they were with us. In fact, day and night they were like a wall of protection to the sheep and to us. You need to know this and figure out what to do, for there is going to be trouble for our master and his whole family. He's so ill-tempered that no one can even talk to him!"

He is right, of course. I thank him and tell him to wait. My mind spins in a hundred directions. Nabal will miss anything I take from the storehouses, but I have no choice. I cannot let David come back, for surely such a hostile response from my husband would ignite David's anger . . . I stop my thoughts before they can go on. Revenge, even to a violent, angry man, is not for me to decide. God has graciously protected me most of the time, and I have learned to deal with this man.

I can only hope that God will deal with Nabal in His way and His time. But I cannot let David do so. David is God's anointed, if the rumors are true. If he is to be king, he will regret hurting innocent men.

I must go to him with food. That should appease him, for undoubtedly his men are hungry and find food hard to obtain. I will also take the blame for my husband. I know it is not my fault, but what else can I do?

## What We Know

When I wrote about Abigail's story for the Wives of King David series, I portrayed a woman who had suffered abuse—physical, verbal, and emotional. I believe that Abigail did suffer in her marriage to Nabal because of the way he is described in Scripture. Nabal did not treat anyone well, and how much his surly, cruel, foolish, and perhaps narcissistic personality affected her, we can only speculate, based on the few things she says.

For instance, when she took food to David, she did not tell her husband, and she asked David to remember her when he came to power. Was she hoping that by then she might be free of her marriage? Or was it a more generic request?

Her motives are something that I can speculate about in fiction, but God's Word doesn't tell us what they are. Yet Abigail is held up as someone many people want to emulate. Is that because of her grace in the midst of a hostile situation? And how do we follow her example?

First of all, I need to say that I cannot relate to Abigail in an experiential way. I have never lived with an abusive man or felt trapped in my situation. I have not experienced what some of my friends have, fearing even being in their husband's presence or afraid to sleep at night for what he might do to them. I've known at least three women who have told me their husbands raped them, and some in gruesome detail. But hearing someone else's story is not the same as living it. I don't have a psychology degree, and while I can imagine a lot, living through the hell some women do is way outside of my ability to comprehend. I am appalled that so many women suffer in this way. I wish it were not so, and I wish I had answers.

For those of you in impossible home situations, my best advice is that you try to get counsel. If you are in danger, there are places that can help.[1] Please seek help if you need it.

So what did Abigail do when she dealt with two very different types of angry men? I think her actions can teach us a lot, even if our cultures are different. But how do we apply her actions, her circumstances, to ours?

The Bible tells us that Abigail was both beautiful and intelligent. I suspect she knew how to use both to her advantage. I do not mean to suggest that she flaunted either, but a beautiful smile or expression can help defuse a negative situation. And she was smart enough to know how to approach the seemingly

1. There are many organizations that give online advice or have a hotline to call. In an abusive emergency, call 911. The website https://www .womenshealth.gov/relationships-and-safety/get-help/state-resources lists agencies state by state, and the National Domestic Violence Hotline is 1-800-799-7233.

inapproachable. I suspect her faith played a big part too, as we see in her speech to appease David. She knew the Lord, and she appealed to David in His name. But first she had to know what was going on.

Paying attention matters when a storm is brewing. If we don't listen to the weather reports, we won't hear that a tornado is barreling right for us, so we won't take cover.

If we know that someone is planning to do another person harm and we say nothing, are we innocent? I know that schools take the word of students seriously today. It wasn't the same when I was growing up—we didn't have such fear in school—but we live in a different world today. Now, if a boy or girl makes threatening comments in school toward teachers or students, that child is going to be dealt with. Our words matter.

In some countries that goes way beyond what is said in schools. People who live in a dictatorship dare not speak against the government or the prevailing religion or pretty much anyone. They might get put in prison or be killed. It's not easy to live in such places.

We don't realize how much it benefits us as a nation to have the freedom to assemble and protest in a peaceful way. We can speak up against the things we don't agree with, though even in the United States some of that freedom of speech is being hindered. Anger abounds, and it doesn't seem to be getting better with time.

That's kind of what Abigail was up against. Her husband's servant came to tell her that David was headed straight for them to kill Nabal and his household. Abigail was caught in the middle of two angry men.

I would not have wanted to be in that position. But she thought quickly, and then she acted.

Abigail knew she was not going to be able to give away a lot of food to David and his men and never tell her husband. He was a wealthy man, and wealthy men tend to keep track of what they own. Some of them can be pretty stingy about keeping their wealth rather than sharing it with those in need. Nabal was one of those people.

But Abigail knew she had to give David food. After all, that was what he'd asked for. To give him platitudes or empty words wouldn't fill one hungry belly, let alone six hundred of them. So she probably had a servant she could trust load donkeys with a lot of food and then followed them to meet David herself.

Nabal had no idea what Abigail was doing, and she didn't tell him. She tackled the most immediate threat first. And she crafted words to David that blessed him so that if the food was not enough, perhaps her speech would be. In that speech, she took the blame for the way his men had been treated.

Note that she didn't take the blame for Nabal's actions. She went so far as to call him a fool, which he was. But she took the blame for not knowing sooner. She hadn't been aware of David's men's visit. If she had, she would have sent them away with plenty.

Sometimes we need to accept blame for things even if we are not in the wrong.

Does that trouble you? Most of us would refuse to apologize or speak humbly to someone we have trouble dealing with, especially if we could not see anything we did wrong.

Imagine you are in a situation where you are held at gunpoint or someone you love is being held hostage. People who try to talk down hostage takers use appeasing language. They will say things to agree with the person holding the weapon, even if those things aren't true. I'm not saying that lying is good. But when you are trying to defuse a volatile situation, carefully choosing your words matters.

Abigail's humility did defuse David's anger, and he praised her. He went away without acting as he had intended. Mission accomplished.

That's the goal in dealing with angry people—especially when anger isn't their normal response. You are more likely to be able to defuse a situation if you are dealing with a reasonable person, as David was.

So many things can cause anger, can't they? Everything from running late and not finding the car keys to being yelled at for something you didn't do to finding yourself the brunt of someone else's problems. Like Abigail. David wasn't her problem. He was Nabal's. But he became her problem when she learned he was going to kill her household.

Abigail dealt with the biggest threat first: David. Once he was appeased, he went back to his hideout. Abigail went home to her angry, proud, mean, possibly abusive, and narcissistic husband. And she intended to tell him what she did.

Do you ever wonder why she told him? Why not just hope he didn't notice? I think she wouldn't have wanted one of the servants blamed for her actions. The blame for the loss of food rested on her shoulders, and she took it.

However, she didn't apologize for what she had done. Why not? In her husband's eyes, she was in the wrong. But in God's eyes, she was in the right. She had obeyed God rather than men, because David was God's man and she knew God was with him. She knew her husband was not walking in obedience to God or His law, and by turning the hungry away he was actually breaking His law. God made provision for the poor and needy, and Nabal refused to help.

Also, when Abigail told Nabal, she did so strategically. She was not about to tell him when he was drunk, which he was by the time she got home. She waited until he had sobered up the next morning. She also didn't apologize to him or beg his forgiveness or fall on her face before him. The Bible only says "his wife told him all these things" (1 Sam. 25:37 NIV).

I wonder if Nabal's anger is what caused his heart to fail and his body to become like a stone. Did he have a heart attack? A stroke? Had he been about to attack Abigail for what she had done?

We are only told that ten days later he died. And David praised God for avenging him against his enemy. I'm pretty sure he was also glad that it hadn't been him who killed the man.

We don't know how Abigail felt about her husband's death. We do know that she accepted David's marriage proposal after Nabal died.

I've talked to women who were relieved when they were no longer married to their abusive husbands, either through divorce or death. It is possible that Abigail felt some sense of relief to be free of Nabal. If you are free of a similar situation, please do not feel guilty for feeling relieved. You are not the guilty party. But I can almost guarantee that you would benefit from some wise counsel. Please, please seek it.

(Side note: If a man or woman has a temper that flares, but they are appeasable and don't take it out on you, they probably need to go to anger management classes or a counselor and get to the root of their anger. Anger does need to be dealt with, because it isn't like aged cheese or wine—it doesn't get better with time. The longer it's held, the more toxic it gets.)

If we have allowed anger to settle in our hearts, it can turn into bitterness. The Bible says that even going to bed angry can give the devil a foothold in our lives (Eph. 4:26–27).

We have to deal with anger. We can't let it fester. If we do, it can have devastating consequences.

I don't want to sound trite in this, because there are fewer situations in families that are more serious than abusive or addicted or angry people. The enemy wants to divide families, and he will work in any way he can to destroy ours. Too many are trapped in dire circumstances.

I think Abigail might have been just as trapped. I think it is possible that she faced a big risk to her own safety by telling Nabal that she did what he had refused to do—show kindness to David. She couldn't undo it and knew she'd done the right thing, but now her life was at risk as she delivered her news to Nabal.

## Imagine with Me

The light from the sun has dimmed significantly during my trip to appease David, and I'm grateful for the servants who accompany me home. If I dwell on it too much, I will admit that talking with David was so much easier than dealing with Nabal when he is in a foul mood, which is most of the time.

My racing heart begins to calm as I feel the donkey move with a steady rhythm beneath me. Appeasing David caused me anxiety, for how was I to know what kind of man he would be? He has killed thousands upon thousands in battle, and I suspect that running from King Saul has not kept him in the best of moods. But I know he is also a man after God's heart, and if he would not kill the king when he had the chance, he wouldn't kill my husband or the servants in our household if I could appeal to the reasonable side of him.

Nabal, on the other hand, I know. Too well. For so long. And I will tell him what I have done because he will find out one way or another, and I cannot risk him taking out his anger on the servants. He could punish everyone, thinking they all told me. Or he could hurt those who helped me.

The setting sun kisses my face, and I feel as though I have been given a touch of grace. God is my refuge and strength. I was thrust into this marriage by my father, and I would have told my parents of Nabal's abuse if I could have. Though if he had lived, my father would have sent me back to Nabal. He would not have believed me over the man who had paid so much to have me.

A sigh lifts my chest. It matters not, for he and my mother are dead, and there is no one else to run to.

I thank God that He has kept Nabal from me more times than I can count. Suffering his anger is something I will never forget. I am only grateful that it is not daily, even weekly. Mostly he grows violent when he's been drinking. And even he knows better than to drink every day. The wine would run out and then he would be worse. He knows how to keep the storehouse full between the wine pressings.

How will I find him when I arrive tonight? I can imagine as the lights of the house come into view. Sheep shearing is always a time when he overindulges. I will not tell him tonight. Tomorrow when the wine has gone out of him will be time enough. I dare not wait longer.

*Oh, Lord, protect me from him. Protect the servants too.*

The donkey draws near the barn, so I pull the reins and he stops. A servant appears and takes the animal to rub him down and feed him, while I walk slowly, praying silently, toward the house.

The noise of celebration greets me, and I enter through the back door. My maid approaches.

"Is he drunk?" I meet her gaze.

"Most completely, mistress. He is very drunk." She shudders, and I wonder if all of the servants are keeping far from him.

"Stay out of the room where he is with his men. Let one of them fill his cup. Go to bed." I wave her toward her room, and she hurries off.

I turn toward my chambers without her assistance. I want to be alone, and the fewer people who know I am here, the better. The men will not look for me. But each step away from the noise only reminds me what I have to say to Nabal tomorrow. I wonder if I will sleep at all tonight.

## From Captivity to Freedom

We are fortunate that in most countries and cultures today, fathers do not choose mates for their children or force them to marry against their will, though there are places in the world where this is still in practice. In fact, there are some cultures that are very oppressive to women.

In our modern American culture, it can be hard to understand Abigail's circumstances. When we fall in love and marry, most of us believe we are marrying a spouse who will always love and be kind to us. But even an intelligent woman can marry a man without realizing he has a brutal temper or is an abuser.

I sometimes wonder if abusive spouses even realize they are abusive in the beginning. While in this case I'm talking about male abusers and female victims, there are female abusers and male victims too. Anger and violence, like adultery and addiction, are not exclusively male or female sins. But from what I've read, most abusers, like Nabal, are men. I wish I could tell you what makes them that way and that they can be healed, but like a drug addict or alcoholic, a person who abuses or bullies others has to want help before they can be helped. And their victims do not have to wait around while they seek it, especially when their own lives or the lives of their children are in danger.

Coming from a Christian, the suggestion of leaving an abusive marriage might not sit well with some believers. But just because we cannot point to one specific verse against abuse does not mean that the message isn't there in the whole of Scripture. God rescued His people from oppressors. He tells us to do the same. To speak up for those who can't speak for themselves. That comes in many forms for many types of victims.

Abigail likely didn't have a way out. If her father still lived, she might have been able to return home, but since she didn't appear to try that, it is possible he was no longer living. Perhaps she had no male relative to defend her.

As I said above, Abigail dealt with David's anger differently than she did Nabal's. She didn't try to appease Nabal, possibly because she knew he could not be appeased. She just told him the truth and waited to see what he would do.

She didn't cower. She didn't run. She didn't lie. She didn't back down. She spoke. And she waited. Perhaps she was waiting on God.

God did come through for her and struck Nabal, who died ten days later. We can speculate about that too. Plenty of abused women probably wish God would do the same to their husbands. But God doesn't go around stopping abuse that way today. In fact, I wonder if Abigail was the reason God struck Nabal at all.

Could He have done so because Nabal had insulted the Lord's anointed? Not to say that God wasn't also protecting

Abigail, but I wonder if David was His primary reason for ending Nabal's life. David was the man through whom the Messiah would come, and God continually had His protecting hand on him.

I don't think women living in situations as tough as Abigail's or worse can look at her and think that's what God needs to do for them. God did protect Abigail by ending Nabal's life, just as He also protected David from any retribution Nabal might have taken had he lived. God put a stop to that right there. He does have a way of dealing with anger.

What if you are living with an angry man? How do you know when to stay and when to go?

If your husband gets angry and can be appeased or left alone to cool down on his own, then he is just a normal person. Everyone gets angry from time to time. If he is not verbally, emotionally, physically, or psychologically abusive to you, then perhaps you can suggest he seek counsel for excessive anger.

Knowing when to stay and when to go is something you need to discuss with a trusted person educated in the field of counseling—unless you are in imminent danger. Then going immediately is necessary. However, if you can make a plan to leave, that is a better goal so you can get safely away. Again, seek counsel or call the hotline I mentioned previously.

Will God be angry with you for leaving? Doesn't He hate divorce? What about submission?

God made exceptions for adultery and unbelieving spouses. He also sent judges to rescue His people from oppressors. In Deborah's day, Sisera was a raping, pillaging, murderous man, and God dealt with him. God does not like it when people mess with those He loves. Please take comfort in that.

This has been a complicated chapter to write. Learning from Abigail and trying to apply what she did to our lives today isn't as easy as it may sound. Sometimes we have to be strong and not allow the angry person to twist our words. We have to know who we are in Christ and cling to that identity. Men like Nabal would try to steal our identity, and Abigail didn't let him do that. She knew who she was and did what she had to do.

She also knew that she needed to obey God, not Nabal. I can hear complaints from those who took a vow to obey their husbands. That doesn't apply if he is asking you to disobey God, and not if his actions would cause harm to someone else you can protect—like your children.

God put protections in the law for women even back in Old Testament times. And Jesus lifted women in the eyes of His culture even higher. If Jesus tells us to bring the little children to Him, and He let women sit and learn at His feet along with the men, don't you think He cares about all of us equally?

God did not make men to be slave masters over women. They were never meant to have such power over their wives. They're supposed to cherish their wives as they do their own bodies. They're supposed to treat their wives with loving-kindness.

Nabal was nowhere near the kind of man who did that. So Abigail dealt with him as best she could. But eventually she did leave, and she married David after Nabal's death. Her life got easier in regards to fear for her safety. But she also had a new challenge—to live in a polygamistic household on the run from a mad king.

## Ponder This

When we are forced to deal with angry people, we need to consider our approach. Are they someone to be reasoned with? Will a conversation and perhaps a gift of kindness help? Sometimes we don't know. I've had kindness backfire. Gifts don't always appease. We can be at a disadvantage if we don't know what the person is like or how they might react. Abigail took a risk with David based on what she knew of his character compared to Nabal's. And she likely prayed as she prepared to appease him.

When we are stuck in a situation where the angry person cannot be appeased, where any attempt to work things out will only escalate the anger, the better solution is to back away. We might need to set up boundaries, or we might need to run the other way. Until we are faced with that kind of situation, it might be hard to know.

Romans 12:17–19 tells us,

> Repay no one evil for evil, but give thought to do what is honorable in the sight of all. If possible, so far as it depends on you, live peaceably with all. Beloved, never avenge yourselves, but leave it to the wrath of God, for it is written, "Vengeance is mine, I will repay, says the Lord."

*If possible.* Sometimes it's not possible to live peaceably with all people. There are some Nabals out there who are angry and abusive. You could go beyond spousal struggles to bullies at school or work, road rage, or violent protests and other uprisings . . . Pick your anger.

God exacted vengeance against Nabal for his mistreatment of David and possibly for what he would have done to Abigail and others in her household. God knows. He sees. And He avenges.

God also rescues. He uses people to help sometimes, as when Abigail helped rescue David from his own anger. Other times He steps in and does the rescuing all on His own.

One thing is certain. God is able to save. He is able to free us from our anger and heal those who are willing to be healed. He is also able to help us flee from the dark places where we find ourselves. Whatever our dilemma, our trial, our devastating circumstance, God is able. He is there, and He is often waiting for us to call on Him to help. And to trust Him to do so.

## TAKING IT FURTHER

1. Have you ever been in a situation where you had to deal with an angry person? How did you handle it? Were you able to defuse the situation? How?
2. Have you been in a bullying or abusive situation? If you are married to an abusive spouse, do you agree that leaving is a biblical option? Why or why not?
3. Do you believe that God wants us to stay in relationships that go beyond simple temper flare-ups now and then? Why or why not? Do you see Him as a God who is willing and waiting to rescue? If so, how?

# Dealing with Heartache

*(Based on 2 Samuel 13)*

## If I Were Ahinoam

I miss the spring flowers in the Jezreel Valley. The red anemones and the purple wildflowers made the fields rise with color and scents and beauty that made my heart glad. I loved the fields, and I think I began picking flowers for my mother's dyes by the time I could walk. She struggled to bring me into the house again, for I loved the outdoors.

Sometimes I wish I could return to what used to be. Mostly I ask myself over and over again, *Why? What did I do wrong? Why did I marry David in the first place?*

My life has been nothing but heartache since that first month of our marriage. I would have requested to go back to my father if I had known what was to come.

I walk to the window in my apartment set along the court of the king's harem. The view shows the distant mountains, and my back door opens to a garden, one of many the king has placed throughout the palace.

King. When we wed, David was on the run from King Saul. There was no assurance that he would ever wear the crown during all of the years we lived in caves and then in the land of the Philistines. Times grew even bleaker when the Amalekites kidnapped Abigail and me and the rest of the women and children, until at last David rescued us. When Saul was dead, we could barely comprehend it. At last we were headed to Hebron, where David was crowned king.

During those years in Hebron, life seemed good. I gave birth to Amnon, David's firstborn, and felt a sense of pride that he looked on me with greater favor after our son's birth.

But the feeling soon fled as David acquired more wives, had more sons, and I felt myself slipping away from him day by day. He never loved me like he did Michal. I was a replacement wife. But at the time, he captivated me and I didn't care.

I wish I didn't care now. Oh, how I wish I could undo what has happened. Is it my fault?

I turn back to this apartment where I have lived since moving to Jerusalem. Amnon used to play in that far right corner of the sitting room. My memory travels to the joy he brought me then. I never did have another child, for David took to his other wives and concubines, and once he married Bathsheba, none of us saw him often.

I want to blame myself most of the time, but I can't bear the guilt. That's when I turn to blaming David for what happened to my son. If he had not lusted after Bathsheba and taken her when she was the wife of another, Amnon would not have gotten the idea that he could take his half sister without benefit of marriage to her.

A shudder rolls through me. Tamar is so wounded. We all felt it when she stumbled into the court of women and her mother took her to her brother's house. Absalom is David's favorite, even over his firstborn, and I suppose I have always felt a hint of jealousy toward Maacah because of it. Amnon is David's heir apparent, but after what he did to Tamar . . .

I turn away from this room, from the hunger for those long-ago memories when my son was small and safe from the temptations of youth. David should have found a wife for him years ago. David. Always too busy chasing after women instead of concerning himself with his sons, their futures, and securing wives for them. What kind of a father ignores his own children?

I move to the courtyard where several of David's wives have gathered in the center, the noise of their chatter grating my ears. A glance my way and they stop. They are talking of Amnon, no doubt. Or me. Do *they* blame me for my son's actions? I had no idea he even cared for Tamar. I could not have imagined that he would take her virtue and send her away. I still find myself reeling from that thought.

*Oh, God, what is to be done to him?* By law he could be stoned. His fate rests in the hands of his father. Will David kill his firstborn for violating his daughter?

I turn away from the women, suddenly sick inside. I cannot bear to speak to a single one of them, not even Abigail, the only wife of David I trust. I find a sense of comfort in seeing that she is not among the gossips here.

I close the door and feel gloom settle over me. I slump into a chair and wave my maid away. I long to weep, but I cannot even feel. My heart is broken beyond repair. Broken for my son. Fearful of what will become of him. Shattered that he could do such a thing.

Again I blame myself, because a mother should know these things, shouldn't she? Someone should have stopped him. Why couldn't I?


## What We Know

Ahinoam is an obscure woman of Scripture. At least we know her name, unlike Job's wife, Noah's, Manoah's, or others in the Bible. But all we are really told of her is that she came from Jezreel, married David after he lost Michal, was kidnapped by the Amalekites along with Abigail, and bore David his first son, Amnon.

Amnon grew up and lusted after his half sister Tamar. She and his half brother Absalom were the children of Maacah, whom we will discuss in the next chapter. Amnon pretended to be sick as an excuse for why he didn't come to court one day, and on the advice of a cousin he tricked his father into sending Tamar to bake cakes for him. (Apparently cake makes you better?) Strange request, in my opinion. I'm rather surprised David agreed to it. Didn't he think it odd to send his virgin daughter alone to bake for her brother? Perhaps David reasoned that Amnon's servants were good enough chaperones—if he even considered Tamar's safety at that point.

Whether it made sense or not, David sent her and she went. And when the moment was right, Amnon sent his servants away and raped his half sister. But unlike his father, who took Bathsheba outside of marriage and eventually married her, Amnon sent Tamar away. Scripture tells us that he hated her more than he had loved her.

But rape is not about love or even lust. It's about power, and maybe Amnon was really making a power play over Absalom to assure himself the throne. Though I wonder if the man had sense enough for that.

Whatever the reasons for Amnon's actions, this is Ahinoam's claim to fame. She was David's second wife and became the mother of a rapist.

I can relate to feeling as though I could have done more, done better as a parent, because none of us are perfect. But I have no idea what it would feel like to have a child who raped a woman or joined a gang or killed because they wanted to see what it felt like. We see these types of people in our society all the time. There doesn't seem to be a single day that passes when we don't hear about a kidnapping, a mass shooting, sex traffickers, a serial rapist, a murderer, or, on a greater scale, the terrorist attacks all over the world. Innocent people are slaughtered in the name of . . . what? I wonder if the terrorists even know why they are fighting. Ideologies are like that. They create havoc in our thinking, especially those that carry a radical bent.

Some of us can relate to such loss because we've been there. Some have lost relatives or other loved ones to violence.

What does it feel like to be the parent of someone who would run people over with a truck in the middle of a celebration? Or blow up runners in a marathon? The list of atrocities is endless, isn't it?

Our society has seen a lot of evil. Every society has. My husband and I were watching a documentary involving Nazi Germany preceding World War II. A lot of news clips were shown that made Hitler sound pretty good to people, even to the church leaders of his day. Except for a few preachers who were actually paying attention, such as Dietrich Bonhoeffer.

Few others spoke against Hitler at the time, just as few people who live in oppressive nations dare speak against their governments today.

Jesus told us there would be evil days like this. He himself lived in evil times under the oppressive regime of Rome. Evil has been with us since the Garden of Eden, and it's not going away until Jesus comes again. It's going to get worse, not better. That is not a comforting thought. With every emerging generation, we think we can fix the brokenness of this world, but no one can. No one ever has, because governments and social ills can't be permanently fixed until God fixes the heart and soul of each one of us.

Rape wasn't new when Amnon raped Tamar. History is marred with a lot of horror. Men have always wanted to control other people. Women were often oppressed, though today we are fighting against that in both good and not-so-good ways. We as women need to take care that we don't end up wanting to hold power over others in even worse ways than it has been held over us. We become no better than our male counterparts if we do.

But back to Ahinoam. She wasn't the one who stole Tamar's virtue. Do you ever wonder how she felt when she heard the truth? Did she plead with David to spare her son's life, when she knew he deserved to die? Or did she simply wait to see what would happen? Did she blame herself for Amnon's choices?

I can imagine that she felt deep agony over her son. If she loved him at all, what else could she feel? She might have blamed herself or his father. Would she have blamed her son or excused him?

If you are a mom, do you blame yourself for choices your children make—especially if you would have chosen differently?

Have you ever put yourself in the shoes of the mother whose son or daughter has done some of the things mentioned above?

I have seen parents forgive the killer of their child, but the parents of a villain often seem to hide from the world. Sometimes they will give an interview, but can you blame them if they don't? It takes courage to share your hurt, and even more to share it publicly. Carol Kent did so in her book *When I Lay My Isaac Down*. She wrote about her only son and how he killed the father of his adopted daughters. His sentence was life in prison without parole. I don't know if that's changed or if it is even possible to appeal.

As I read Carol's story and heard her speak about it, I realized that she was taking a pretty big risk sharing her heart. And it's not an easy story to digest, especially if you think about your own kids as you read it. What if I had to go through that with one of mine? I cannot even imagine.

Maybe that's the point. Ahinoam was a rather tragic character in the story of David's life. If David had not committed adultery and murder, would his son have had the audacity to rape his sister? Are the sins of the parents put on the children? The Bible tells us that each person answers for their own sins (Deut. 24:16; Jer. 31:30; Ezek. 18:19–21).

That tells me Amnon was the one responsible, not Ahinoam. No matter what type of mother she was, she was not the only person raising her son. And despite the penchant today to blame parents for more than they deserve, I don't think we can fairly or accurately do so here. We weren't there. We didn't see what went on. And God didn't tell us. We do know that even more tragedy followed this one. Ahinoam suffered more than anyone would want to bear.

So what *can* we learn from Ahinoam's life? Is there any good we can draw from her?

## Imagine with Me

The sky is dark, the clouds gray and threatening, as though to remind me of all I've lost. Was the day this dark when my son died? I pull my knees to my chest and curl into a ball. I do not want to see the light. My mind drifts, and I pray for oblivion. May I never see the light of day. Oh, that I had died in my mother's womb and never known earthly joy, for there will never be good in my life again.

A knock on the door pulls my thoughts up from the abyss, but only slightly. I still crave the darkness and refuse to open my eyes, even as I vaguely hear the door open. Is that Abigail's voice in the distance? Footsteps draw closer. A touch on my arm barely registers.

*Let me die with him.* Oh, that I had died instead of Amnon.

"Ahinoam?" Abigail's soft voice begs a response, but I offer none. "Ahinoam, you must rouse yourself. You cannot stay in this room in the dark forever."

*Yes I can. If I die here, they will just move me to a darker place. A fitting end to my useless life.*

"Ahinoam, please." Her hand moves up and down my arm, and I feel the sensation stronger now. "Come back to us. I miss your company. No one blames you for what Amnon did or what Absalom has done. Even Maacah is distraught over his actions. Please, my sister, come back to us."

Has David been here and said similar words? I cannot recall if he came. How long has my mind shut down from the world around me? I attempt to open my eyes, but my lids will not lift. Perhaps it is for the best.

"She's not responding." Abigail's hand lifts, and I feel her pulling away. "I don't know what else to do."

A deeper voice answers her. "I had hoped . . ."

*David? Is that you?* I want to rise, to shout at him and ask him why he allowed Amnon to go with Absalom to a remote place where there would be no one to protect my son. Hadn't David known this was possible? That Absalom would avenge Tamar because their father had done nothing?

But the words will not move past my throat. My mind screams his name. *Amnon!* My heart yells at David, for I blame him for it all.

"If she will not wake and eat, she will die," David says to Abigail.

The words comfort me. If I can just stay in this place of deep darkness and refuse food, I will soon join Amnon. Then I can be with my son again.

I hear footsteps and a door close. They have left my maid to watch what I will do. But I have made my decision. I will not awaken if I can help it. I am as dead as if Absalom's men have thrust me through too. I welcome it. For without my husband's love or my son's presence, I have nothing left.

## When the Pain Is Great

In this second book about Bible women, I wanted to encourage and uplift each reader. I sought to show us all—myself included, for I learn as I write—the good things they learned, the trials they survived. And maybe Ahinoam's outcome was the complete opposite of what I have imagined here. She could have survived the death of her son. I have friends who have lost children and lived full lives, even though there is a hollow place left by their loss.

But as I imagined Ahinoam's whole world, I wonder if she had the strength of those I know who have loved and lost. She never struck me as a strong woman, not even when I wrote about her in the Wives of King David series. Perhaps I am wrong. I hope I am.

Let's look at this, then, from both sides. When the pain is great, even if it is not the kind of loss Ahinoam suffered, what do we do with it? How do we survive the agony?

Sometimes as a writer, I receive comments or letters from people who have suffered much loss. Children lost to an accident or suicide, spouses who die too soon, or the estrangement or heartbreak of broken families. I wish I had comforting words to say. Sometimes all I can do is offer a hug.

But from these people, I see two responses. We can grow stronger or we can give up. Pain rarely leaves us the same person we once were. If Ahinoam had grown stronger, perhaps she could have reprimanded Amnon after what he did and convinced him to marry Tamar. If that didn't work, perhaps she would have appealed to David to force them to marry.

In this day and age, I would *never* suggest a woman marry her rapist! But back then it was a thing. Tamar even suggested it because she knew that no other man would have her and she would die without children in her brother's house. That fate was worse than marrying a man like Amnon.

I know, it was a strange world and had strange customs that we don't always understand. All of this was before Jesus elevated the role and place of women in society, so keep that in mind.

If Ahinoam had been a strong woman who allowed her trials to make her better instead of hopelessly bitter, she might have grieved Amnon's death but survived it. She might have found other ways to use her talents and her time. The unfortunate thing is that the Bible doesn't tell us. We can only surmise what happened to her.

I wrote the negative, tragic ending to her life here because that is our second choice. And it does happen, doesn't it? In Ohio, one state away from me, there is an opioid crisis that is claiming the lives of many people. Social drinking among Christians is far more acceptable than it was even twenty years ago. Tobacco companies are considering restricting the age of vaping to twenty-one because teenagers are getting hooked on tobacco and are causing harm to themselves. According to the CDC, "Since 2008, suicide has ranked as the 10th leading cause of death for all ages in the United States. In 2016, suicide became the second leading cause of death for ages 10–34 and the fourth leading cause for ages 35–54."[2]

I can bet every one of us knows at least one person who has taken his or her own life. I know of three, and that's without thinking about it very hard. So it's a possibility that someone facing what Ahinoam did might want to give up.

Job's wife wanted him to give up when they lost everything, including their children. Job told her she was talking foolishly. But imagine being in her shoes. Job was suffering, but she was their children's mom! Her suffering had to have been enormous.

We don't know if Ahinoam ever had another child besides Amnon. He is the only one mentioned. If she'd had other children, she might have found worth in living for them. But if she was living in a harem, was not her husband's favorite, and had lived through her son's awful choices and then his murder, well . . . how would you feel?

I don't want to know how I would feel. I don't want to imagine such tragedy and loss. That's why I don't want to ever

2. Holly Hedegaard, Sally C. Curtin, and Margaret Warner, "Suicide Mortality in the United States," 1999–2017, CDC, November 2018, https://www.cdc.gov/nchs/products/databriefs/db330.htm#ref1.

write about Job! But my heart goes out to those of you who just might have suffered something close to this. Who felt like you just couldn't take it anymore. And who might have considered ending it all.

That is easy to relate to for many of us. Depression is rampant today. It's why every doctor asks if we're depressed every time we visit. It's rather annoying to be asked that over and over, but they're worried about those suicide rates that keep climbing. I get that. And I get what it feels like to be in a deep, dark place in life. But the good news is that we don't have to stay there.

Jesus came to do more than raise the role of women in society. He came to give each one of us eternal life if we will believe in Him, entrust our lives to Him. Will that stop the trials and tragedies? No. They could actually get worse. Comforting thought, I know. But our Good Shepherd walks with us through the valleys. He offers grace to get through the tough times. He pulls the wayward from the pit they are in and the abandoned from the slavery of self-pity. He knows how to heal the human heart.

That's what Ahinoam needed above all else. She needed her broken heart to be healed. We know that David found healing for his sin and the pain he'd caused others, because he wrote psalms about his struggles. But we can't know if his wives or children did.

Yet we can know that God is there, waiting to heal our broken hearts. He is holding out His hand to take ours and walk with us through this troubled life. He's pulled me out of many a pit, and He keeps doing it because I tend to trip over my melancholy emotions too much. I need His grace to find joy again.

How about you? If you are facing trials like Ahinoam did, are you going to allow them to make you stronger, or will you give up and remain in a broken state? We have a choice. All it takes is for us to cry out to God for rescue. I've called on Him many times, and He is right there. He might not change my circumstances, but He always works to heal my heart.

## Ponder This

We are not given any guarantees that everything we ever hope for will happen. Life in this broken world is flawed, and it always will be until Jesus returns to set things right again. Sin has marred the joy and beauty God always intended for us. While Ahinoam and women like her throughout the ages have suffered immeasurable loss, there is a God who came to redeem that loss, to set us free from the depression or vices that hold us captive. If we but ask Him to.

> Whoever dwells in the shelter of the Most High
> will rest in the shadow of the Almighty.
> I will say of the Lord, "He is my refuge and
> my fortress,
> my God, in whom I trust." (Ps. 91:1–2)

God can and will be our refuge, our strength, our deliverer in times of trouble. He longs for us to call on Him because we love Him. If we love Him, we will discover how much He delights in us. That doesn't mean we won't fail Him or wander or doubt. But the deep, dark places need not hold us when He has us in His mighty hand.

Even if we as believers succumb to desperation due to some tragedy, as Ahinoam might have done, God will never abandon us. He knows we are dust, and He is a merciful, loving, forgiving God. He will also rescue and save those who believe. Our future can be bright despite the pain, despite the broken world. Count on it.

## TAKING IT FURTHER

1. If you had lived in Ahinoam's circumstances, how would you have reacted to the actions of your son? How do you think the parents of children who commit heinous crimes feel? Do you think they are to blame for their children's actions? Why or why not?

2. Given what the Bible tells us about Ahinoam, how do you think she might have handled the news that her sister-wife's son had murdered her son? In a sense, it is not much different than Cain's murder of Abel. What would you do if one of your children seriously harmed their brother or sister? How would you advise someone else to act if they were in a similar situation?

3. Do you believe there is redemption offered to people who rape or murder or commit any other heinous crime? Can God's love truly cover every sin? Why do you think we struggle to accept that evil people could one day find salvation and forgiveness? Can you forgive those you might blame for the circumstances of your life? Why or why not?

## When Life Is Out of Control

*(Based on 2 Samuel 3; 13; 15)*

### If I Were Maacah

The emissaries of David, the new king of Israel, surprised me. How quick they were to agree to a marriage alliance between a princess of Geshur and this new king. Of course, I had no choice but to agree when my father chose me for the honor, but I wondered then, as I wonder now, if this marriage is really an honor at all.

The ride from Geshur to Hebron took longer than I had hoped, and the sight of Hebron's town caused a sour note in my spirit. Such a backward place and much smaller than I had imagined. My father had warned me that David was not yet the king of all Israel, only the tribe of Judah, so I should not have been surprised at the small quarters. I did not like them,

163

for I had left a grander palace under my father's rule. And I had looked forward to becoming first wife of a great king or at least a high-ranking noble. I did not expect to be David's third wife, and him just out of exile.

A deep sigh lifts my chest as I walk the gardens in the house given for our use here. One of the residents freely gave his spacious home to David when they crowned him king. But we have no palace here, and I am cramped in quarters that barely rank above a servant's.

"Hello, Maacah."

I turn quickly at Abigail's greeting. Among David's wives, she is the easiest to speak to.

"Abigail. I see you are as bored as I am today." Why else would I walk the gardens? There is simply nothing to do here.

"Oh, I am not bored," she says, smiling.

I stiffen, for though she says it kindly, it feels as though she has reprimanded me.

"I just needed a break from weaving. I am making David another new robe, fit for his office as king."

"I don't weave." I don't mean to sound as though such work is meant for servants, but I cannot help myself. Such work *is* meant for servants, and the wives of the king should not have to do such things.

"I could teach you. You would be less bored." She steps closer and then bends to pick an anemone and holds it to her nose. The scent wafts to me, and she tucks the flower behind her ear. "Weaving is an art, not simply a task for those who serve us," she says. "I have learned to create the softest linens and to weave thread through the finished garment to put David's symbol and other embroidered designs along the edges."

The thought does not appeal to me in the least, but I lift a brow and give her a curious look to hopefully show interest.

"You must show me what you have done. But I would think that the king would hire the best artisans to make his clothing. Why would one of his wives do such work?"

I don't mean to cause her mouth to draw into a tight line. Abigail is always so gracious. I want to take back the words, but that is something I never do.

"You must remember," she says, "David lived in the wilderness for ten years. He was a shepherd before he was a king, and Ahinoam and I are not of royal blood. But we married him before he was king. You have an advantage over us in that you come from a king's palace. You know better than we do what a palace should be like."

I stare at her for a lengthy breath. "Show me your work. And perhaps you can tell me more of our husband and his life in the wilderness." I am far more interested in David than I am in weaving, and what better way to learn of him than from the women who have been with him the longest?

I don't expect her comments to matter to me once David truly knows me. I will learn what I can about his past, but then I will use it to make him see the advantage I have over them. As nice as Abigail might be and as quiet as Ahinoam grows from time to time, they can't actually have captured David's heart. I am far more beautiful, if the silver mirror speaks truth. Soon David will realize that I am also far more interesting.

Whatever their history with him, I will win his heart. I will not have to compete for his time and affection. Who knows? I might even convince him to think himself in love with me. Then however many children I bear him will become his favorites.

Abigail can have her weaving. I will surpass her in every other way.

## What We Know

Maacah is another woman in Scripture who gets very little page time. We know her name and the names of her children and her father. Why her father is named isn't clear, because when Solomon married the Egyptian princess, we are not told which pharaoh was her father.

Maacah was a princess of Geshur, daughter of Talmai, its king. She had two children with David that we know of—Absalom and Tamar. It is possible she had others.

That is all the Bible gives us about Maacah, other than she married David when he was the king of Judah, and he reigned in Hebron before he became king of all Israel and relocated his capital to Jerusalem.

Maacah's son, Absalom, was probably David's favorite. I wouldn't be surprised to learn that David intended Absalom to rule after him. The Bible doesn't tell us that, but David seems to have greater affection for Absalom than his other sons until Solomon is born.

After Absalom and Tamar are born, however, we don't hear much about them until after David's adultery with Bathsheba. Once that affair, the murder of Bathsheba's husband, and the death of their child occur, then Absalom's and Tamar's stories are given to us in Scripture. While David had other daughters, Tamar is the one whose story is better known than her mother's.

The story is a tragic tale that begins with Amnon's lust for his half sister Tamar and his later rape of her, which I covered in the previous chapter. Tamar is shut out of Amnon's house afterward and walks through the streets in mourning. The next thing we read is that Absalom tells her to keep quiet about it, and she eventually resides in his house. Two years later Absalom kills Amnon.

Absalom, who runs to his grandfather Talmai after Amnon's murder, remains exiled there but later returns to Jerusalem. There is a rift between him and his father, but eventually he is restored to court, where he begins his next plot, to usurp the throne and kill his father.

So here we have Maacah in the middle of all this, assuming she was still alive. Imagine that she was still living in David's household. How would she have comforted her daughter after such an incident?

Have you ever known someone who was raped? Perhaps that person is you, in which case, may I offer my support and sorrow for what you've been through? I have not lived through that tragedy, but it is a horrible thing and shouldn't happen to anyone.

What if you haven't experienced that either, but suddenly you are faced with the fact that it just happened to your daughter, your granddaughter, your friend, your friend's daughter? What do you do? What do you say? How would you encourage your child or your friend and help them survive such a thing?

I can imagine the way Jesus would have reacted because of who He is. He looks upon people with love and great compassion. He is the one who touched the leper and allowed the broken woman to weep at his feet. He ate with the despised and called the outcasts to be part of his inner circle.

Jesus would grieve about rape just as much as you and I would. In fact, I know he would be angry at such sin. He has a protective heart toward victims of oppression. We see this throughout Scripture. God answered the cries of the oppressed. He made provision for the orphan, the widow, the foreigner. And people who were victimized, like Tamar, had to break His heart.

Based on how Jesus might act and how He acted in Scripture, I think we need to treat an abuse or rape victim with compassion, not judgment. Rape is never their fault. Remember, it's an act of power, not lust, not love. While the victim will feel shame, and others might even accuse them of "asking for it" based on how they were dressed, no one ever "asks" for it. They are not guilty. Period.

So please, let's have no judgment in our churches or our Bible studies or our friendship circles. And no gossip. If this is really your friend—or worse, your child—you want to help wherever you can. Get them to or encourage them to seek medical help and counseling. Be there if they want to talk, but understand if they don't. Keep their confidence. A silent presence might be all they need. Watch for signs of depression, and do all you can to see that they receive help to get through this. Rape will haunt them for the rest of their life. Even if the pain lessens, they will never forget.

For a woman of Tamar's day, rape meant she was ruined and most likely would never marry or bear children. Such a condition would make her feel disgraced. Today we make no such stigma that prevents marriage or future relationships, so it's harder to relate to Tamar's circumstances.

I mention Tamar and Absalom to help us understand or imagine what their mother might have felt, given what happened to both of them. How does a mother act when her daughter is treated so cruelly?

I think in Maacah's place, I would have held Tamar close and wept with her. I can imagine feeling immense anger at Amnon, and I might even march into David's audience hall or private quarters and demand to know what he was going to do about it.

I'm the protective type, and even with sons, I felt protective. They're my kids, after all. When one is hurt or wounded in some way, I want to fix it. I bet Maacah wanted to fix her children's situation too. But she was not the one to fix anything. Absalom, on the other hand, had a plan to do just that.

## Imagine with Me

There is news, and I find myself rushing to the courtyard with the other women, heart pounding. David often met with his children here when they were young. Now his sons are grown with homes of their own, though some have not yet married. Only Bathsheba's sons remain at the palace, but David keeps them set apart from us.

The resentment of that favoritism still stings, but I tamp down the anger as I lean closer to the servant, straining to hear.

"News has come from the house of Absalom," the eunuch says.

I push my way forward. "What news?" Why am I left in the dark about my son's actions?

"Absalom has had his brother Amnon killed with the sword. The rest of the sons of David have fled, and Absalom has escaped to Geshur." The man looks at me, and I feel my skin tingle and heat at the same time.

Beside me, Ahinoam falls to her knees, weeping. "No! No!" She screams her son's name over and over again, and I back away from her, unable to bear it. Abigail catches my glance, but I turn and hurry to my rooms, where Tamar has remained these past few months.

"What is it, Ima?" She rises from the couch where she spins thread in a room too dark for this time of day. How small she has seemed these past two years since Amnon defiled her. Absalom took her in until two months ago when he said he was having his home worked on—adding an addition for his sister and me, if David will allow me to leave. Of course, we all know that David will never allow such a thing.

But I take comfort in knowing that my son will care for Tamar when I am gone, because I do not trust her father to do so. If David had cared to protect my girl, he would have executed Amnon two years ago.

I close the door and move to the couch, beckoning her to join me. "It seems that your brother has taken vengeance on Amnon and has ordered him killed. But of course your father will not react well, so Absalom has gone to Geshur. My father will protect him there while David gets over his anger. We must keep our distance from your father in the meantime."

"My father rarely visits us anyway. I have not seen his face since it happened." She looks at her feet as she always does when she speaks of what Amnon did to her, which is rarely. It is as though she blames herself for Amnon's treachery, but I blame her father and Amnon. She is an innocent victim, but no one treats her thus except her brother and me.

"Will he be gone long, Ima? Do you think my father will allow him to return soon?" She meets my gaze, longing in her dark eyes. My children have always been close, but this has made them closer. What will I do without Absalom to comfort her? To comfort us?

"I do not know, my daughter. Can you not hear Ahino-am's screams for her son? No doubt the king is equally grief-stricken. And no doubt angry that your brother would take justice into his own hands."

"Absalom would not have even considered doing so if my father had acted first." Tamar lowers her gaze once more, and I sense despair and sadness overtaking her again.

If I could appeal to David to bring my son home or let us go to him, I would. But David will mourn Amnon, his firstborn, whether he should or not. And in some part of my heart, I know my husband feels responsible for Amnon's actions because of his adultery with Bathsheba.

The sons grow bolder when the father's actions are weak. And despite God's apparent forgiveness of David, Absalom sees his father as weak. I do not disagree with him.

### From Disbelief to Acceptance

As we discussed in Ahinoam's chapter, parents of adult children are not responsible for the choices those children make. They might have been good parents whose kids grew up and decided to follow a path they weren't taught. Or they might have been not-so-good parents whose kids either followed their footsteps or instead decided to be better and take a different path, for good reason. In any case, adult children are responsible for their own decisions, good or bad.

So even though we might look at Amnon as a rapist or Absalom as a murderer, we cannot claim that Ahinoam and Maacah were the cause of their bad behavior. But can we blame David? Should we blame anyone?

Some people point to David's sin with Bathsheba and say that Amnon would never have had the audacity to rape his sister if he hadn't seen his father take another man's wife and do something similar. Perhaps Absalom would not have killed Amnon if not for seeing David get away with killing Bathsheba's husband, Uriah.

And yet, Amnon's lust for Tamar was not contingent on David's lust for Bathsheba. Each man's heart is his own. Each man's proceeding actions also give us a glimpse into his character.

David treated Bathsheba with greater kindness and respect after he repented than Amnon treated Tamar, and with Amnon there was no repentance.

The same was true for Absalom. He went on to deceive his father and lead an army against him in an attempt to kill David and take his throne. Absalom's resentment led him to some atrocious acts.

I wonder if Maacah knew about Absalom's desire to kill Amnon. Had he spoken threatening words in her presence? Even if he had, could she have done anything? Warned anyone? The Bible doesn't tell us. But if I had walked in her shoes, I imagine I would have been conflicted, and perhaps I might have wanted revenge or at least justice done to the man who wronged my daughter.

Once Amnon was dead at her son's hands, did it give Maacah peace? Or did she walk around in a state of disbelief for a long time?

During her years of marriage to David, she must have kept in contact with her father in Geshur, for Absalom knew where to flee when he needed to get away. Did Maacah plant that idea in his mind, or might Absalom have come by it naturally, given his mother's close connection to her father?

And when Absalom came after David, how must Maacah have felt to be running from her own son with a husband she may or may not have respected at that point? Did she go back to her father? Would David have allowed her to do so, given the circumstances?

There is a lot of speculation here, I know. But there are two things I hope we can learn from Maacah's situation:

1. We are not in control of our children's choices. With young children, we as parents do have the right to

guide them and teach them as they grow up. We want to raise responsible, loving children. We also want to protect them, but that only goes so far. God alone is sovereign and the only true refuge in times of trouble. We can run to Him and trust Him, but we can't control our world or the outcome of whatever situation we find ourselves or our children in.

2. Because we are not in control of others, the only thing we can do to help them is to focus on changing ourselves. If we want to be more loving or less critical or less sarcastic and cynical, then we need to do something about that. This is especially true when our children are young because we are setting an example for them. If we want them to mimic our behavior, we best make sure our behavior is worth mimicking. Do we have a critical, judgmental spirit? Our children might develop one as well.

Is our home the most loving and caring we can make it? Children *are* affected by our attitudes and behavior. My husband sees this at the junior high level nearly every day when he substitute teaches or volunteers at the local school. (He's retired from his previous job.) Some kids are very troubled, and they act out with bad behavior. Often these kids have no guidance at home and no one who really cares about them.

I hope Maacah was not that type of mother. David wasn't the most attentive father, at least to some of his children. I do hope the mothers tried to make up for any lack the children might have felt. But even if Maacah was the best mother in the world, Absalom was still bent on revenge. When his world was going well, he was probably the darling of the court. But when Solomon came along and Tamar's rape was not avenged, things changed. Or perhaps Absalom had always planned to kill Amnon, no matter what his father decided.

Absalom and Tamar, like Maacah, lived a life of privilege. They all held the role of son or daughter of a king. And it is possible they all enjoyed favoritism from those kings. But what may have started out as favoritism toward Maacah and later her children ended in heartbreak and tragedy.

Can you relate? I can't relate to tragedy of this magnitude as a wife and mom. But I do understand heartache. I think everyone can relate to that, because at some point in life we've all been wounded. Some of us have been wounded by our own children, like Maacah was. Or someone else mistreats our children.

Parents don't go through life without experiencing something that hurts them. No one tells you that when you're pregnant. No one tells you that when your children are small either. Though I do recall being told, "Little kids, little problems. Big kids, big problems." And then your kids grow up and you outgrow your job. They don't tell you that either!

I loved being a mom. Raising kids was one of the greatest pleasures of my life. I struggle to understand people who don't enjoy their kids, or who mistreat them or don't want them around or can't wait until they turn eighteen so they can move out. That never made sense to me. How can you not love your own children?

But some people do not love anyone, and that can hurt us whether we are young or old. One thing to remember in all of this is that God loves us through everything. He loves us through our failures, our successes, our joys, our sorrows. He sees. Even if it feels like everyone has rejected us and no one cares, He cares. He always has. He always will.

## Ponder This

Wherever life takes us—whether we face good things and find favor in the eyes of all, or we feel as though no one will ever love us—never forget God. Never forget the lengths to which Jesus went to win our hearts. Never forget that He came for the sole purpose of restoring our relationship to His Father so we could be with Him forever.

No matter how far we may think we have fallen, how guilty we may feel over someone else's sin, or how angry we are over treatment we receive, God is waiting to heal us. He could have healed Maacah's broken heart, Tamar's wounded heart, and even Absalom's angry heart—if they had let Him.

That's the key. Jesus never forces His will on anyone. He loves people, and He wants us to believe that He is who He says He is. He wants to heal us, to free us, to save us from ourselves. But we have to ask Him. We have to want Him.

> The Lord is not slow in keeping his promise, as some understand slowness. Instead he is patient with you, not wanting anyone to perish, but everyone to come to repentance. (2 Peter 3:9 NIV)

Only God knows a person's heart. We cannot know what other people truly believe or even what they choose about God when it comes to life's end. We are responsible only for ourselves. We are not in control of our children's choices, but we are in control of our choice to believe. May today be the day we do just that.

## TAKING IT FURTHER

1. What do you think of Maacah? For a time her children were possibly among David's favorites. How do you think she felt when Bathsheba's children usurped hers?

2. Have you ever known someone or the parent of someone who was raped or murdered? Have you known the parent of one who did such a thing? If so, what can you do to be a friend to them as they face these or other tragic circumstances?

3. Do you think parents are responsible for the choices of their adult children? The argument of nature vs. nurture says that children are either born the way they are going to be or they are a product of their environment. Which do you think is true? Is it both? Why or why not?

# Bathsheba

## Learning to Forgive

*(Based on 2 Samuel 11–13)*

### If I Were Bathsheba

My sandals brush the mosaic tiles covering the palace floors, my heart and mind struggling with yet another tragedy. Amnon has raped Tamar. How could he? I am not yet over the loss of my son or my husband, and yet I am thrust into the king's grief and inability to do anything to make the situation right.

David. So sure of himself the night he called me to his bed and the day he had my husband killed, until at last Nathan confronted him and he faced his sin. Why did our son have to suffer for David's sin? And now his daughter suffers too.

*Why, Lord?* Surely I must have committed some awful sin to be put in this place. I respect the king, I tell myself, but I wish I had held the courage of Abigail and refused him that night. None of this would have happened if not for my weakness.

Hurried feet sound behind me, and I turn. My rooms are in that direction not far from the king's. I expect to see a guard, and my heart jumps as I wonder what else may have befallen us. But it is only Tirzah, my maid. I breathe a sigh and smile as she approaches. Tirzah has been with me through everything.

"Mistress." She stops and lowers her head in a slight bow. "I did not expect to find you so quickly."

"I only recently left my rooms." I continue toward the larger palace gardens. I need to take in the fragrant air of the outdoors, away from the cloistered feeling in the palace.

Tirzah hurries to walk beside me. "I wonder," she says, bold as she always is, "if you might talk to the king about Tamar. Perhaps he would listen to you, force Amnon to do the right thing."

"The right thing would be to have his firstborn son killed, Tirzah. The king cannot bear to do such a thing. He has barely recovered from thinking about our child. Forgiven by God or not, we both still grieve." The truth is, David has come to me only once to comfort me since our son's death. A son we never even had the chance to name, for he died seven days after his birth, one day short of his circumcision and naming.

A sick feeling fills my middle, and I hold a hand there to still the slight nausea. After David came to me, Joab called him away to finish the war that had killed my husband. A few months have passed, and now this with Amnon.

"Is there no way to insist he marry her or find an honorable man to take her instead?" Tirzah, always the hopeful one, carries a practical streak and loves to fix my problems. She can't, of course, but she has been with me since my mother's death, and I rely on her wisdom to help me. She alone knew about my night with the king—until the pregnancy. Then there was no way to hide it.

"No one will marry a tainted woman." I look at my maid as we stop at the entrance to the gardens. "Well, I suppose that's not entirely true." David married me, after all, but it was his fault I bore that stigma. Had Uriah ever known, even he might not have taken me back. I could be buried beneath a pile of stones if not for David's actions. No, it was God's mercy that we were not both killed. For I didn't speak up to stop him. I just allowed the king to do as he wanted with me, and sometimes I still find forgiving him difficult.

The sick feeling comes over me again. Tirzah looks at me, her gaze scrutinizing. "How long has it been since you were with the king?" She takes my hand and leads me into the garden to a stone bench resting beneath the shade of an almond tree.

I give her a skeptical look. "He came soon after the child died. I have not been with him since he returned from the war. I spoke to him about Amnon, but he is not open to hearing advice from anyone."

"He might listen to you if you tell him you are carrying his child." She patted my hand.

"It's too soon." But I count back in my mind. "It has been nearly two months."

"Have you had your time?"

I have been so busy thinking about my losses and the king's consequences from the Lord, of which Amnon surely is a part, that I have given little thought to myself. "No," I say at last.

"No wonder your stomach gives you such trouble. You are not as much upset about Tamar as you are sick with child." Tirzah smiled. "God has given you another to replace the child who died for David's sin."

179

"*My* sin," I say. "Had I insisted he stop . . . I gave in to him, Tirzah. I was attracted to him and couldn't say no."

"So you were both at fault, but God held David responsible, did He not?"

I nod. "Yes." But I had known in my heart that I needed to repent and had done so as well.

"If God can bless you both after what the king did against Him, surely He can redeem what Amnon did if the king will do something. If you tried again . . ."

I hold up my hand. "I have tried, Tirzah. To mention Amnon only brings his anger. He has been to see Tamar, but he feels powerless to do anything to Amnon. How can he force a marriage when his son hates the woman he abused? At least David cares for me. Amnon hates Tamar now that he has gotten what he wanted." I look beyond her at the wispy clouds. "You cannot make someone love another." I glance at her again, and her gaze holds me fast.

She nods. "I wish Tamar could be helped. She will never forgive Amnon, or her father for sending her to his house. How could the king not see?"

I sigh, longing to speak of something else. The truth is, even I struggle nearly every day to forgive David. To forgive myself. David should have seen Amnon's duplicity. What father sends his daughter to bake for a son without guards to oversee things?

But the guards had looked the other way when David invited me to the palace that day not so long ago. David trusted his son as he had trusted his guards to keep his secret. And both Tamar and I had been used in ways we did not invite. But Tamar was far worse off than I.

"David is broken, Tirzah. Even in his worship, his songs carry tones of sadness. He loves Adonai and wants nothing more than to please Him. All of his life, he has loved our God. But he sinned greatly, and no matter how often he reminds himself he is forgiven, a part of him will always remember that he deserved to die. He is a different man than the one who called me to his bed." I realize it more fully as I say the words. Perhaps I need to be more forgiving of him . . . and tell him so.

"Is he no longer capable of leading?" Tirzah whispers and glances around us.

I shake my head. "He is still king, and a good one. But as a father and even as a husband, he feels . . . defeated. As though he will never be able to make things right."

Tirzah touches my middle. "Perhaps this new child will make a difference. Will you tell him soon?"

Should I? The taste of bitterness touches my tongue, but instead of swallowing it back, I close my eyes and ask God to remove it. In that moment, I choose to forgive my husband the king for everything he did to me and against my family, and even for his weakness with his own. He needs me to be strong for him. No other wife can even speak to him right now.

"I will tell him." I stand and smooth my robe. "I suppose there is no better time than now."

Tirzah smiles and follows me into the palace.


## What We Know

The story of David and Bathsheba is well known even outside of Christian and Jewish circles. David earned some negative notoriety during that phase of his life that I bet he wished he could have undone. While much is written of David in Scripture, here is what we know about Bathsheba.

She was the daughter of Eliam, who was one of David's mighty men, as was Bathsheba's husband, Uriah. Ahithophel,

Bathsheba's grandfather, was David's counselor who betrayed him to follow Absalom years after David committed adultery.

We do not know how Bathsheba came to marry Uriah, a Hittite rather than a Hebrew as her father and grandfather most likely were. (In Scripture, only Uriah bears the label "Hittite." If Bathsheba and her father were also Hittites, it makes sense that they would have been designated as such.) We also do not know how long she and Uriah were married, but they did not have children.

Bathsheba came at David's summons to the palace, and there is no record in Scripture that she resisted his advances. One could argue that no one went against the king, but before David was king, Abigail appealed to his common sense and he listened to her. She stopped him from murdering innocent people. Then again, David was king now and his attitudes could have changed. Bathsheba may or may not have attempted to stop the adultery.

She gave birth to a son conceived by David while she was still married to Uriah. God was not pleased with what David had done, and their child died due to their sin. We know how David reacted when he heard the child was sick, but nothing is said of Bathsheba's actions.

As a mom, I can guess how she might have felt or what she might have done. "Mama bear" protectiveness would rise up in a mom whose infant was threatened. Babies are so vulnerable. So when the babe grew ill, we can almost feel Bathsheba's pain. But did she bear guilt for her part in the adultery, or was she angry with David for making her feel like she had no choice? Could she have been bitter toward Uriah for not coming home to cover their sin? Was she afraid of the future, of what would happen to her once the child died? Would David cast her aside? What reason would he have to keep her around with no child? After all, he had killed Uriah and married her because of the child.

We don't know her feelings or thoughts, but it's easy to imagine what they might have been. Did she feel used by David? If she loved Uriah, the loss of both husband and child would have been doubly acute.

I think God gives us a glimpse of her future with these few words after their child dies: "Then David comforted his wife, Bathsheba, and went in to her and lay with her, and she bore a son, and he called his name Solomon. And the LORD loved him" (2 Sam. 12:24).

If David had not gone to Bathsheba to comfort her and attempt to give her another child, her life could have been forfeit. He was her protector now, and this comfort was more than just a way of telling us that they had another baby. David repented of his sin and took responsibility for Bathsheba for the rest of her life. From what I glean from Scripture, just the fact that they had five sons (perhaps daughters too, but they are not mentioned) tells us that he likely spent more time with her than he did his other wives. She may have become his favorite, though probably not his exclusive.

Other than her role in Solomon's rise to power and later his court, we don't know a lot of details about Bathsheba. She strikes me as perhaps timid in the beginning, perhaps even enthralled by the king, but later she learns to navigate her role and grows into a powerful woman, protective of her sons.

The one thing Scripture usually does not tell us in these stories, though sometimes it gives us a glimpse, is how the people feel or what motivated them to act as they did. I like to imagine those things, which is why I normally write biblical fiction. I wrote much more about this story in my novel *Bathsheba*. But for our purposes here, I wonder about Bathsheba's ability or willingness to forgive the people in her life who wounded her or took advantage of her.

Was she happy to marry a Hittite? If not, did she forgive her father for giving her to Uriah in the first place? If she did love Uriah, then she probably had a decent relationship with her father, who would have arranged the marriage.

Did she forgive her grandfather for betraying David to follow Absalom? Her grandfather likely held a long-standing grudge against David for taking Bathsheba, which would give a reason for his decision to follow Absalom. Ahithophel, like Absalom, wanted to see David killed. That's a lot of buried anger.

Ahithophel's life came to a sad end. Did Bathsheba forgive her grandfather for taking his own life once he saw that his advice was no longer being followed? If someone close to you has committed suicide, you know there will come a point where you have to forgive him or her for that. The truth is, we often have to forgive any person for dying. It's part of the grieving process.

I think the main person Bathsheba might have had to forgive besides herself (because we often beat ourselves up the most) was David. Put yourself in her shoes a moment. Would you have been angry with the man who put you through so many negative, loss-filled circumstances? I would have. Even if I had struggled with Uriah's devotion to his men, I wouldn't have wanted him to die. No one wants to lose a mate—unless that mate is abusive, and then there are circumstances when one might wish to be done with a marriage.

But I don't see Bathsheba in those circumstances. I see a woman who was going through her monthly purification in the privacy of her courtyard, never expecting the king to be on his roof or to see her there.

(Side note: A lot of people say she was bathing on her roof. The Bible doesn't say that. It was typical of that day for women to bathe in the inner courtyard of their homes. So let's not paint Bathsheba as a temptress. She might have been completely innocent at this point. What followed, even if she gave in willingly, ruined a lot of her life.)

Has another person taken advantage of you? Wounded you? Destroyed what you had built of your life? Have you been able to forgive them? How easy do you think it would have been for Bathsheba to forgive all the wrongs done to her?

## Imagine with Me

The walk back from Mahanaim has not been easy, despite the fact that we are returning home to the palace and David is still our king. Absalom, who conspired with many of David's men, including my grandfather, is dead, a fact David has struggled to process. He often walks alone in his grief, though he does allow me to comfort him now and then.

Things grew worse when we learned my grandfather had killed himself. Perhaps it was a just reward for his betrayal, and no doubt David would have had him executed or banished him from Jerusalem for siding with Absalom. Still, I loved my grandfather. Though I know my grief over him pales in comparison to David's grief over his son. I have lost a son too. I know the feeling.

Although . . . perhaps I do not know the feeling quite like David does, for when our son died, David said he would one day go to him, though he would not return to us. But with Absalom, his cries are bitter, though quiet now. His tears carry no hope, as though he does not believe he will see this son again.

That is the worst type of grief.

I walk beside my husband as we enter the palace. At least my father has stayed true to David. For that I am grateful.

But I find myself caught in that web of resentment and hurt all over again. Every tragedy reminds me of those in the past, and I don't want to remember. I want to be free of those burdens. I want the future to hold brightness and hope.

I wish we could go back and undo everything. David would not have suffered so many losses if not for our sin. But I cannot go back, and I know I must accept God's forgiveness of me and of David. And I have no choice but to forgive Absalom, Amnon, my grandfather, and everyone else who has looked at me with disdain.

Surely if God can show mercy to me, I can show mercy to others. Yet I struggle. Bitterness and hurt are so subtle sometimes. They creep into my thoughts unaware, and before I know it, I am angry again.

How hard it is to forgive. And yet how blessed it is, as David has said, to know God's forgiveness! Why am I always torn between the two?

We stop at David's rooms, and I start to move toward my own when his hand clasps my shoulder. "Come, join me, beloved."

I smile at his pet name for me. "All right." I turn back and follow him into his chambers, where so few are allowed to enter.

He seats me among the cushions and settles beside me. One arm about my shoulders, he takes my right hand in his. "I am sorry," he says, as though he has never said the words to me before.

"For what, my lord? You have done nothing to offend me." He knows he has in the past, so I seek to reassure him.

"For everything." He studies my hand and turns it palm up. "This time I am sorry you lost your grandfather. There was a time when I trusted him without question."

"I know." I cup his beard and lean close to kiss him. "While we can both say these things are our fault—they fall on our shoulders—we did not make these people do as they did. We are responsible for our own sin. God has allowed consequences for that, but the choices to do wrong are still Amnon's, Absalom's, and Ahithophel's alone." I brush my fingers through his hair, and he draws me closer.

He kisses the top of my head. "Thank you." I know he means far more than this, but his words will come out in a song or some other writing eventually.

"Thank you" is enough because I know he understands. We, the forgiven, have no choice but to forgive others. We will continue to do so as long as God gives us breath. I think I'm finally beginning to understand that.

## From Wronged to Forgiving

Forgiveness and reconciliation are two themes that seem to come out in all of my books, whether I consciously think about them or not. Perhaps this is because these two things are part of who I am. They are my heart's longing and desire for all—to know God's forgiveness and be reconciled to Him, and then make life right with everyone else as far as it concerns us. After all, we can't make others accept or love us. We can only show them as much love as they allow. The rest is up to them and God.

I don't know whether Bathsheba grappled with the need to forgive, but considering her circumstances, I would not be surprised if she did. Several people wronged her in her life.

When someone wrongs us, we either hold a grudge or forgive. There really are no other options—even if they never know we forgave them, even if reconciliation is not possible. Forgiveness is for us. It releases the hold that those who hurt us have over us. Without forgiveness, the hurt never quite goes away. With it, the joy of reconciliation could happen. But forgiving our past has to happen first.

I wonder how many of us struggle with the hurts and wounds of our past. I used to. Sometimes I still do, if a new wound surfaces that reminds me of something long forgiven. But I've learned that a grudge—allowing the sun to go down on our anger—gives bitterness a foothold in our hearts. The longer it lingers, the more it grows beyond a foothold. Pretty soon, bitterness grows and turns everything in our lives sour.

We've all known bitter people. One thing that is true of all of them? They are not happy. I've been that bitter person at times, and believe me, it does not add to my happiness.

But sometimes our wounds aren't as obvious as Bathsheba's pregnant belly. Sometimes they happen so subtly that we do not even realize we are bitter or angry. And anger and bitterness go hand in hand—just sayin'.

When I was young, something didn't go the way I expected it to, and it hurt my feelings. The other person had no idea I felt hurt, and I didn't say anything about it. I didn't pray about it or forgive the hurt. I just stuffed the emotion inside and forgot about it. (Bad idea.)

Fast-forward about fifteen years. I began experiencing physical issues that had no easy solution. It sounds like my life today with chronic pain, but I'm beginning to figure out some of the things that cause that. This was different. And I wanted to understand why it was happening to me.

What came out of my search to understand was the memory of that long-ago day when I stuffed that hurt. And with it came a number of other memories of people toward whom I was holding grudges. It's interesting that when we begin to pray and let God reveal truth to our hearts, He slowly reminds us—not all at once, but one by one—of things that are blocking our relationship with Him and with other people we love. We are hurting ourselves the most when we cling to past hurts that are forgotten by everyone but us.

God taught me how to release those things and forgive what was past. Since I often wrote in my journals at the time, He coaxed me to compose a letter to the people who had caused me hurt, real or imagined. Then I wrote, "I forgive you" all over the paper and burned it. The act freed me from the sin of holding grudges and the symptoms they had caused. It freed me to love the people in my life who had unintentionally wounded me.

We can only speculate about whether Bathsheba held any grudges. Since such things are so common to the human race, I don't doubt that every one of us faces the need to forgive over and over again in our lives. Until we reach heaven and live joyfully in the kingdom of God, we will struggle with our reactions to life's circumstances. And God will ask us to forgive again and again. Seventy times seven. And beyond.

**Ponder This**

The psalmist (possibly David) wrote this in Psalm 130:3–5:

> If you, O LORD, should mark iniquities,
> O LORD, who could stand?

> But with you there is forgiveness,
>    that you may be feared.
> I wait for the LORD, my soul waits,
>    and in his word I hope."

And Matthew 6:14–15 says,

> For if you forgive others their trespasses, your heavenly Father will also forgive you, but if you do not forgive others their trespasses, neither will your Father forgive your trespasses.

I think forgiveness is a big deal to God. After all, He sent His Son to earth to die on a cruel Roman cross, lie in a tomb for three days, and rise victorious over death and sin simply to be able to offer us forgiveness for our sins against Him. And our sins are more than we usually realize.

It takes humility to admit that we are sinners. It's not a popular teaching or a popular word today. Too many would rather toss God aside and live like He doesn't exist than have to look in the mirror and face the truth that they are flawed. None of us are born into this life perfect, nor will we ever be able to live up to what God's glory requires. Not apart from Jesus Christ.

When I wrote *Bathsheba*, I'd read a lot about her life and other novels about her. In at least one case, Uriah was blamed for not being an attentive husband, which caused Bathsheba's eyes to wander. The writers seem to want to excuse what David did by placing some of the blame on the innocent party—Uriah.

As I pondered her story, I talked about some of this with one of my sons, who was still living at home at the time. He said something I will never forget, and I chose to follow his advice. "Don't make light of the sin," he said.

Yet how often do we do that? We make light of sin when we stuff it down and hold a grudge, knowingly or not. We make light of it when we blame other people for our own actions. We make light of it when we refuse to see that we are sinners in need of a Savior.

When we are tempted to hold on to hurts and make light of our own sins of holding grudges or being unwilling to forgive, let us keep in mind that our God sees all. He knows our thoughts before we think them. He knows our words before we say them. He knows why we suffer. He knows when we forget Him or choose blame or some other excuse to keep the truth from touching our hearts. He knows.

But even in knowing us better than we know ourselves, He holds out His offer of forgiveness. If you haven't taken that offer yet, I pray you will. Then turn around and offer it to someone who has wronged you. Such action pleases God, and we will be happier in this life when we do so.

## TAKING IT FURTHER

1. Do you find it easy to forgive someone when they wrong you? Do you hold a grudge, or are you quick to apologize or forgive? Why?

2. Do you think Bathsheba struggled to forgive David for all that happened to her after he coaxed her into adultery? If you could rewrite her story, what might it look like?

3. Forgiveness and reconciliation are my two favorite themes, as I said before. What themes run through your life? Is there someone who needs your forgiveness and reconciliation? Will you take that first step to repair what is broken?

# CONCLUSION

As I've mentioned, this book was not easy for me to write. I wanted to offer a more positive spin on each of these women than I had on the women in *When Life Doesn't Match Your Dreams*. The trouble is, Scripture gives us more about the difficult things that happened to them than the good things, depending on the woman. And then there was the problem of not having experienced anything like what some of them went through. I can get away with that in a novel, but here, not so much. So my editor and I decided to change the heading "In Our World" to "What We Know" for each woman, first because I wanted to stay true to what the Bible says about her, and second because in many cases I couldn't relate very well and didn't know anyone in those circumstances.

I thought the wives of King David would be easy to tackle because I knew David's story so well. But Abigail, Ahinoam, and Maacah ended up being the hardest to write about. As I said in Abigail's chapter, I haven't lived with a Nabal—abusive, in my opinion—so I took the angle of her appeasing angry men. Ahinoam was the mother of a rapist. I cannot understand what that would be like, nor do I know anyone who can. If you are one of those mothers facing such circumstances, please know that you have my deepest empathy.

Maacah was the mother of a rape victim and a murderer. As I mentioned in that chapter, I know of one person whose son killed another, but can you imagine the hurt Maacah must have felt in seeing her children suffer so? Any mom can relate to that, I think.

So you can see my dilemma—at least, I hope so. That's why this book is more like a Bible character study than the last one. I do hope it helps you to understand these women of Scripture better, and perhaps in doing so helps you understand yourself a little better too.

Thank you for taking the time to read this book. I hope the stories blessed you.

In His Grace,
Jill Eileen Smith

# ACKNOWLEDGMENTS

No book, fiction or nonfiction, would ever make it to the shelves without the help of a fine team of people behind the author. Even independently published books need editors and designers and ultimately readers!

I would like to thank the many teams at Revell—editorial, marketing, publicity, design, and more. For this book I had two acquisitions editors—Lonnie Hull DuPont and Rachel McRae. And Jessica English, my line editor, always makes my pages shine.

Melissa Anschutz and Olivia Peitsch make a wonderful publicity and marketing team. Thank you to both of you.

Gayle Raymer—Thank you for another great cover!

Wendy Lawton—This series began with your faith in the project. Thank you for always believing in me.

Hannah Alexander—Thank you for reading this one before it went off to publishing. I appreciate your friendship most, but your encouragement made this book better.

Friends—Thank you to those who have prayed and those who have listened to me verbally pace in frustration over how to craft these words.

Family—Randy, you are my heart. Jeff, Chris, Molly, Keaton, Ryan, Carissa, and Jade, you mean more than words can say.

As always, I am ever grateful to Jesus, my Savior Messiah, for spilling His story all through the pages of the Old Testament and weaving His being into the lives of these people so that we could learn from their stories. One day I long to be with You and to meet all of them.

**Jill Eileen Smith** is the bestselling, award-winning author of the Wives of King David, Wives of the Patriarchs, and Daughters of the Promised Land series, as well as *The Heart of a King*, *Star of Persia*, and the nonfiction book *When Life Doesn't Match Your Dreams*. Her research has taken her from the Bible to Israel, and she particularly enjoys learning how women lived in Old Testament times.

When she isn't writing, she loves to spend time with her family and friends, read stories that take her away, ride her bike to the park, snag date nights with her hubby, try out new restaurants, or play with her lovable, "helpful" cat, Tiger. Jill lives with her family in southeast Michigan.

Contact Jill through email (jill@jilleileensmith.com), her website (www.jilleileensmith.com), Facebook (www.facebook.com/jilleileensmith), or Twitter (www.twitter.com/JillEileen Smith).

## Meet
# JILL EILEEN SMITH

at **www.JillEileenSmith.com** to learn
interesting facts and read her blog!

## Connect with her on

 @JillEileenSmith

# ONLY GOD CAN
# HEAL OUR HEARTS

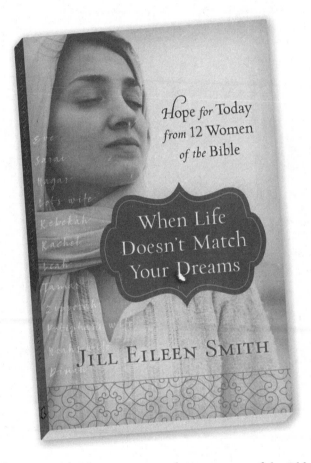

Drawing on her extensive research into women of the Old Testament, novelist Jill Eileen Smith turns her pen to what we can learn about trusting God from women of the Bible. And you'll come away with the confidence that God loves you and is forming you through your trials into the woman He longs for you to be.